W9-APA-225

Front Cover Artwork: *The Bookworm*
(German: *Der Bücherwurm*)
1850 oil-on canvas painting
by Carl Spitzweg
(February 5, 1808 - September 23, 1885)

Cover design by Michael Bourgeous

Quotes of Note:
Brilliant Thoughts
Arranged by Subject

Edited and Composed by
Brogan L. Fullmer

Quotes of Note: Brilliant Thoughts Arranged by Subject
Copyright © 2005-2014 by Brogan L. Fullmer

All rights reserved.

Electronic Edition for Amazon Kindle Wireless Reading Device Copyright © 2010-2014

The Amazon Kindle is a registered trademark of Amazon, Inc.

All trademarks are property of their respective owners.

With
grateful acknowledgement to
Fran Zedney
and
the wonderfully talented staff of the Stewart Library
of
Weber State University

This work is dedicated to those who seek the daily progress and betterment of human civilization. May humanity remember that which it values and protect that which it loves.

-Brogan Lee Fullmer

"The nicest thing about quotes is that they give us a nodding acquaintance with the originator which is often socially impressive."

-Kenneth Williams, 1926-1988

Table of Contents

Table of Contents

Table of Contents

Table of Contents

xii

Table of Contents

Table of Contents

xiv

Table of Contents

Table of Contents

Explanation of Formatting

Author's notation

-Believed to be said by First Middle "Nickname" Last, suffix [legal or married name], noble title in language of title, year of birth-year of death

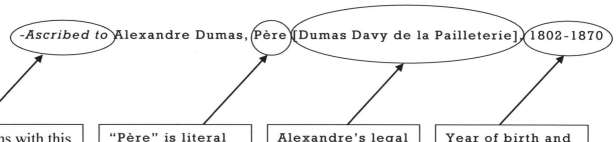

-*Ascribed to* Alexandre Dumas, Père [Dumas Davy de la Pailleterie], 1802-1870

Quotations with this prefix denote no known reference for the quote or of the author saying it.

"Père" is literal French for "Father." Other authors may include "Fils,"(literal French for "Son") "Sen." (Senior) or "Jun." (Junior).

Alexandre's legal name given at birth. Many authors use pen names or change names in life.

Year of birth and year of death. "c." implies "circa," literal Latin for "around." Others used are "B.C." implying "Before Christ" and "A.D." implies "Anno Domini" literal Latin for "Year of Our Lord." A.D. begins immediately following 1 B.C.

Noble Titles and Monarchs

All noble titles of authors are included after an author's full name, separated by a comma, and before the author's year of birth and death. A monarch is listed by their royal name, such as Elizabeth II.

In the Peerage of the United Kingdom, the ranks of the peerage are:

1. Duke
2. Marquess
3. Earl
4. Viscount
5. Baron

Peers of the United Kingdom are often hereditary and include a number of the person to hold the noble title, such as "1st Duke of Wellington." Most continental peers do not have a number of inheritance.

In the Peerage of continental Europe, most ranks of peerage are:

1. Duke
2. Marquess
3. Count
4. Viscount
5. Baron

Ability

See also Art, Talent

"What it lies in our power to do, it lies in our power not to do."

-Aristotle, 384-322 B.C.

"I have learned to use the word impossible with the greatest caution."

-Dr. Wernher Magnus Maximilian von Braun, Freiherr von Braun, 1912-1977

"When you are unwilling to sacrifice or conceal any of your abilities their reputation is generally diminished."

-Luc de Clapiers, Marquis de Vauvenargues, 1715-1747

"A professional is someone who can do his best work when he doesn't feel like it."

-Alfred Alistair Cooke, 1908-2004

"There is great skill in knowing how to conceal one's skill."

-François VI, Duc de La Rochefoucauld, 1613-1680

"To measure up to all that is demanded of him, a man must overestimate his capacitates."

-Johann Wolfgang von Goethe, 1749-1834

"There is no need to show your ability before everyone."

-Baltasar Gracián, 1601-1658

"No matter how far a person can go the horizon is still way beyond."

-Zora Neale Hurston, 1891-1960

"A man may be so much of everything that he is nothing of anything."

-Dr. Samuel Johnson, 1709-1784

"A single pomegranate seed suffices to reconstruct a ruined world."

-Arabian proverb

"If you can't bite, don't show your teeth."

-Yiddish proverb

"Ability is what you're capable of doing, motivation determines what you do, attitude determines how well you do it."

-Anonymous

Achievement

See also Failure, Success

"All rising to great place is by a winding stair."

-Sir Francis Bacon, 1561-1626

"Woman inspires us to great things, and prevents us from achieving them."

-Ascribed to Alexandre Dumas, Père [Dumas Davy de la Pailleterie], 1802-1870

"It is the end that crowns us, not the fight."

-Robert Herrick, 1591-1674

"Whatever the mind of man can conceive and believe, the mind can achieve."

-Napoleon Hill, 1883-1970

"It's not the mountain we conquer, but ourselves."

-Ascribed to Sir Edmund Percival Hillary, 1919-2008

"Those that have done nothing in life are not qualified to judge of those that have done little."

-Dr. Samuel Johnson, 1709-1784

"The way to get things done is not to mind who gets the credit of doing them."

-Ascribed to Benjamin Jowett, 1817-1893

"The father of every good work is discontent, and its mother is diligence."

-Lajos Kassák, 1887-1967

"Many a crown shines spotless now that yet was deeply sullied in the winning."

-Johann Christoph Friedrich von Schiller, 1775-1854

3

"People of accomplishment rarely sat back and let things happen to them. They went out and happened to things."

-Ascribed to Elinor Smith [Elinor Regina Patricia Ward], 1911-2010

"Knowledge may give weight, but accomplishments give luster, and many more people see than weigh."

-Philip Dormer Stanhope, 4th Earl of Chesterfield, 1694-1773

"Footprints on the sands of time are not made by sitting down."

-Anonymous

Admiration

See also: Fame, Flattery, Glory, Praise, Respect

"Egotist, *noun*. A person of low taste, more interested in himself than in me."

-Ambrose Gwinnett Bierce, 1842-1914

"A fool always finds a greater fool to admire him."

-Nicholas Boileau-Despreaux, 1636-1711

"When you can do the common things of life in an uncommon way, you will command the attention of the world."

-Ascribed to George Washington Carver, 1864-1943

"Ignorance is the mother of admiration."

-George Chapman, 1559-1634

"When we feel that we lack whatever is needed to secure someone else's esteem, we are very close to hating him."

-Luc de Clapiers, Marquis de Vauvenargues, 1715-1747

"We always like those who admire us; we do not always like those whom we admire."

-François VI, Duc de La Rochefoucauld, 1613-1680

"I have always been an admirer. I regard the gift of admiration as indispensable if one is to amount to something; I don't know where I would be without it."

-Paul Thomas Mann, 1875-1955

"The most respectable women are the most oppressed."

-Mary Wollstonecraft [Mary Wollstonecraft Godwin], 1759-1797

Adultery

See also: Deception, Lies, Morality, Sin, Truth, Trust, Vice

"So heavy is the chain of wedlock that it needs two to carry it, and sometimes three."

-Alexandre Dumas, Fils 1824-1895

"To look for discretion in a first love is irrelevant. First loves are accompanied by a joy so excessive that it must be allowed to overflow or it will stifle a man."

-Alexandre Dumas, Père [Dumas Davy de la Pailleterie], 1802-1870

"A man does not look behind the door unless he has stood there himself."

-*Ascribed to* Henri Du Bois, 1863-1918

"The violence we do to ourselves in order to remain faithful to the one we love is hardly better than an act of infidelity."

-François VI, Duc de La Rochefoucauld, 1613-1680

"As a rule, the person found out in a betrayal of love holds, all the same, the superior position of the two. It is the betrayed one who is humiliated."

-Ada Leverson, 1862-1933

"Adultery is the application of democracy to love."

-Henry Louis Mencken, 1880-1956

"A woman we love rarely satisfies all our needs, and we deceive her with a woman whom we do not love."

-Valentin Louis Georges Eugène Marcel Proust, 1871-1922

"A man who marries his mistress leaves a vacancy in that position."

-Ascribed to Oscar Fingal O'Flahertie Wilde, 1854-1900

"Those who are faithful know only the trivial side of love; it is the faithless who know love's tragedies."

-Oscar Fingal O'Flahertie Wilde, 1854-1900

Adversity

See also (Mis)Fortune

"In skating over thin ice, our safety is in our speed."

-Ralph Waldo Emerson, 1803-1882

"When we look into the eyes of another we see opportunity, when we look down on someone we see success, when we look in the mirror we see our adversary."

-John Frederick Charles Fuller, 1878-1966

"Problems are messages."

-Shakti Gawain, 1948-

"He knows not his own strength that hath not met adversity."

-Ben Jonson, 1573-1637

"Mishaps are like knives that either serve us or cut us as we grasp them by the blade or the handle."

-James Russell Lowell, 1819-1991

"Do not rely completely on any other human being, however dear. We meet all life's greatest tests alone."

-Agnes Campbell MacPhail, 1890-1954

"A certain amount of opposition is a great help to a man. Kites rise against, not with the wind."

-John Neal, 1793-1876

"The thorns which I have reaped are of the tree I planted."

-George Gordon Noel, 6th Baron Byron, 1788-1824

"Sleep, riches, and health to be truly enjoyed must be interrupted."

-Johann Paul Friedrich Richter, 1763-1825

"Anyone can hold the helm when the sea is calm."

-Publilius Syrus, first century B.C.

"The mass of men lead lives of quiet desperation."

-Henry David Thoreau, 1817-1862

"If you want to enjoy the rainbow, be prepared to endure the storm."

-*Ascribed to* Warren Wendel Wiersbe, 1929-

"Adversity introduces a man to himself."

-Anonymous

Advice

See also Opinions

"Who cannot give good counsel? 'Tis cheap; it cost them nothing."

-Robert Burton, 1577-1640

"A timid question will always receive a confident answer."

-Sir Charles John Darling, 1st Baron Darling, 1849-1936

"Advice is what we ask for when we already know the answer but wish we didn't."

-Erica Jong, 1942-

"We are generally the better persuaded by the reasons we discover ourselves than by those given to us by others."

-Blaise Pascal, 1623-1662

"Advice is seldom welcome; and those who want it the most always like it the least."

-Phillip Dormer Stanhope, 4th Earl of Chesterfield, 1694-1773

"When we ask advice we are usually looking for an accomplice."

-Charles Varlet, Marquis de La Grange, 1639-1692

"It is always a silly thing to give advice, but to give good advice is fatal."

-Oscar Fingal O'Flahertie Wilde, 1854-1900

Age

See also Children

"The secret of staying young is to live honestly, eat slowly, and lie about your age."

-*Ascribed to* Lucille Désirée Ball, 1911-1989

"Grow old along with me! The best is yet to be"

-Robert Browning, 1812-1889

"Nature gives you the face you have of twenty; it is up to you to merit the face you have at fifty."

-Coco Chanel [Gabrielle Bonheur Chanel], 1883-1971

"Youth is a blunder; manhood a struggle; old age a regret."

-Benjamin Disraeli, Earl of Beaconsfield, 1804-1881

"A person is always startled when he hears himself seriously called an old man for the first time."

-Oliver Wendell Holmes, Sen., 1809-1894

"There are people whose watch stops at a certain hour and who remain permanently that age."

-*Ascribed to* Charles Augustin Sainte-Beuve, 1804-1869

"The closing years of life are like the end of a masquerade party, when the masks are dropped."

-*Ascribed to* Arthur Schopenhauer, 1788-1860

"That sign of old age, extolling the past at the expense of the present."

-Sydney Smith, 1771-1845

"We are always the same age inside."

-Ascribed to Gertrude Stein, 1874-1946

"Old and young, we are all on our last cruise."

-Robert Louis Balfour Stevenson, 1850-1894

"Old age is a high price to pay for maturity."

-Sir Tom Stoppard [Tomáš Straussler], 1937

"No wise man ever wished to be younger."

-Jonathan Swift, 1667-1745

"Cherish all your happy moments; they make a fine cushion for old age."

-Ascribed to Newton Booth Tarkington, 1869-1946

"Old age is the most unexpected of all the things that happen to a man."

-Leon Trotsky [Lev Davidovich Bronstein], 1879-1940

"One should never trust a woman who tells one her real age. A woman who would tell one that, would tell anyone anything."

-Oscar Fingal O'Flahertie Wilde, 1854-1900

"The tragedy of old age is not that one is old, but that one is young."

-Oscar Fingal O'Flahertie Wilde, 1854-1900

"The older the fiddler the sweeter the tune."

-English proverb

"Birthdays are good for you, the more you have the longer you live."

-Anonymous

Ambition

See also: Dreams, Desires, Goals

"Ambition drives the tragic hero into the abyss of his fate, but also marks him as the hero."

-Ascribed to Aristotle, 384-322 B.C.

"'Why not' is a slogan for an interesting life."

-Ascribed to Mason Cooley, 1927-2002

"One must be something to be able to do something."

-Johann Wolfgang von Goethe, 1749-1834

"We will either find a way, or make one."

-Ascribed to Hannibal, c. 247- c. 182 B.C.

"The slave has but one master; the ambitious man has as many as can help in making his fortune."

-Jean de La Bruyère, 1645-1695

"I am not ambitious: at any rate, my ambition is so intimately bound up with my whole being that it cannot be distinguished from it."

-Napoléon I [Napoléon Bonaparte], 1769-1821

"The very substance of the ambitious is merely the shadow of a dream."

-William Shakespeare, 1565-1616

"Don't let young people confide in you their aspirations; when they drop them they will drop you."

-Logan Pearsall Smith, 1865-1946

"Those who are believed to be most abject and humble are usually most ambitious and envious."

-Benedict Spinoza, 1632-1677

"Ambition is putting a ladder against the sky."

-American proverb

"Your current safe boundaries were once unknown frontiers."

-Anonymous

Anger

See also Hatred, Jealousy

"No man is angry that feels not himself hurt."

-Sir Francis Bacon, 1561-1626

"Never forget what a man says to you when he is angry."

-Henry Ward Beecher, 1813-1887

"Heaven has no rage like love to hatred turned, nor hell a fury like a woman scorned."

-William Congreve, 1670-1729

"Anger as soon as fed is dead—'Tis starving makes it fat."

-Emily Dickinson, 1830-1886

"You cannot shake hands with a clenched fist."

-Indira Priyadarshini Gandhi, 1916-1984

"Nothing lowers the level of conversation more than raising the voice."

-Stanley Horowitz, 1925-

"My life is in the hands of any fool who makes me lose my temper."

-Joseph Hunter, 1914-1974

"To be furious, is to be frighted out of fear."

-William Shakespeare, 1564-1616

"Make no friendship with an angry man and with a furious man thou shalt not go; Lest thou learn his ways, and get a snare to thy soul."

-*The Proverbs* 22:24-25

11

Arts

See also Ability, Talent

"An actor is something less than a man, while an actress is something more than a woman."

-Richard Burton, 1925-1984

"Artistic temperament is a disease that afflicts amateurs."

-Gilbert Keith Chesterton, 1874-1936

"Modern art is what happens when painters stop looking at girls and persuade themselves that they have a better idea."

-John Anthony Ciardi, 1916-1986

"Connoisseurs think the art is already done."

-John Constable, 1776-1857

"Criticism is easy, art is difficult."

-Philippe Néricault Destouches, 1680-1754

"Show me a great actor and I'll show you a lousy husband. Show me a great actress, and you've seen the devil."

-*Ascribed to* William Claude Fields [William Claude Dukenfield], 1880-1946

"Be regular and orderly in your life like a bourgeois, so that you may be violent and original in your work."

-*Ascribed to* Gustave Flaubert, 1821-1880

"One must not always think that feeling is everything. Art is nothing without form."

-Gustave Flaubert, 1821-1880

"Art is either plagiarism or revolution."

-Eugène Henri Paul Gauguin, 1848-1903

"There is no work of art that is without short cuts."

-André Paul Guillaume Gide, 1869-1951

"Individuality of expression is the beginning and the end of all art."

-Johann Wolfgang von Goethe, 1749-1834

"The artist who is not also a craftsman is no good; but, alas, most of our artists are nothing else."

-Johann Wolfgang von Goethe, 1749-1834

"Keep to yourself the final touches of your art."

-Baltasar Gracián, 1601-1658

"Were I to proceed to tell you how much I enjoy...architecture, sculpture, painting, music, I should want words."

-Thomas Jefferson, 1743-1826

"Art hath an enemy called ignorance."

-Ben Jonson, 1573-1637

"I think it's bad to talk about one's present work, for it spoils something at the root of the creative act. It discharges the tension."

-Norman Kingsley Mailer, 1923-2007

"The great artists of the world are never Puritans, and seldom even ordinarily respectable."

-Henry Louis Mencken, 1880-1956

"Abstract Expressionism was invented by New York drunks."

-Joni Mitchell, 1943-

"Bad artists always admire each other's work."

-Oscar Fingal O'Flahertie Wilde, 1854-1900

"In the evenings the art of building gave way to that of music, which is architecture, too, though invisible."

-Marguerite Yourcenar [Marguerite Cleenewerck de Crayencour], 1903-1987

"The artist doesn't see things as they are, but as he is."

-Anonymous

Attitude

See also: Beliefs, Doubts, Happiness, Opinions, Sadness, Thought

"A positive attitude may not solve all your problems, but it will annoy enough people to make it worth the effort."

-Ascribed to Herm Albright, 1876-1944

"What you're supposed to do when you don't like a thing is change it. If you can't change it, change the way you think about it. Don't complain."

-Maya Angelou [Marguerite Johnson], 1928-

"When we cannot change a situation, resolution comes through the way we choose to handle it within ourselves."

-Gerald "Jerry" Coffee, 1934-

"A pessimist is a man who thinks all women are bad. An optimist is a man who hopes they are."

-Chauncey Mitchell Depew, 1834-1928

"Nothing great was ever achieved without enthusiasm."

-Ralph Waldo Emerson, 1803-1882

"The greatest revolution in our generation is that of human beings, who by changing the inner attitudes of their minds can change the outer aspects of their lives."

-Marilyn Ferguson, 1938-2008

"I have always preferred the folly of the passions to the wisdom of indifference."

-Anatole France [Jacques Anatole François Thibault], 1844-1924

"The last of the human freedoms is to choose one's attitudes."

-Dr. Victor Emil Frankl, 1905-1997

"The only disability in life is a bad attitude."

-Scott Hamilton, 1958-

"Every extreme attitude is a flight from the self."

-Eric Hoffer, 1902-1983

"What you are capable of achieving is determined by your talent and ability. What you attempt to do is determined by your motivation. How well you do something is determined by your attitude"

-Louis Leo "Lou" Holtz, 1937-

"Clear your mind of can't."

-Dr. Samuel Johnson, 1709-1784

"Since we cannot change reality, let us change the eyes which see reality."

-Nikos Kazantzakis, 1883-1957

"A loving person lives in a loving world....A hostile person lives in a hostile world....everyone you meet is your mirror."

-Ken Keyes, Jun., 1921-1995

"Cynicism—the intellectual cripple's substitute for intelligence."

-Joseph Russell Lynes, Jun., 1910-1991

"How many pessimist end up by desiring the things they fear, in order to prove that they are right?"

-Robert Mallet, 1915-2002

"It's my up, my down. I could choose to see this situation as a setback or a starting point."

-W. Mitchell [William John Schiff III], 1943-

"When a man reaches a condition in which he believes a thing must happen because he does not wish it, and what he wishes to happen can never be, this is called 'desperation.'"

-Arthur Schopenhauer, 1788-1860

"The value of an ideal has nothing whatever to do with the sincerity of the man who expresses it."

-Oscar Fingal O'Flahertie Wilde, 1854-1900

"Idealism is what precedes experience; cynicism is what follows."

-David T. Wolf, 1943-

"It's bad if we want something to stick forever; but good if we want a post-it-note."

-Anonymous

Beauty

See also Image

"Beauty soon grows familiar to the lover, fades in his eye, and palls upon the sense."

-Joseph Addison, 1672-1719

"Beauty is the great seducer of man."

-Paulo Coelho, 1947-

"O, she is the antidote to desire."

-William Congreve, 1670-1729

"Love built on beauty, soon as beauty dies, dies."

-John Donne, 1572-1631

"A beautiful woman should break her mirror early."

-Baltasar Gracián, 1601-1658

"If a man hears much that a woman says, she is not beautiful."

-*Ascribed to* Henry Samuel Haskins, 1878-1957

"What attracts us in a woman rarely binds us to her."

-Cyril Edwin Mitchinson Joad, 1891-1953

"A woman who cannot be ugly is not beautiful."

-Karl Kraus, 1874-1936

"Rarely do great beauty and great virtue dwell together."

-Petrarch [Francesco Petrarca], 1304-1374

"God, in pity, made man beautiful."

-Mary Wollstonecraft Shelley, 1797-1851

"Use harms and even destroys beauty. The noblest function of an object is to be contemplated."

-Miguel de Unamuno, 1864-1936

"All beauty comes from beautiful blood and a beautiful brain."

-Walter Whitman, 1819-1892

Beliefs

See also: Attitude, Doubts, Philosophy, Religion, Thought

"Conscience is thoroughly well bred and soon leaves off talking to those who do not wish to hear it."

-Samuel Butler, 1835-1902

"We prove what we want to prove, and the real difficulty is to know what we want to prove."

-Émile-Auguste Chartier, 1868-1951

"Man is what he believes."

-Anton Pavlovich Chekhov, 1860-1904

"A fanatic is one who can't change his mind and won't change the subject."

-Sir Winston Leonard Spencer Churchill, 1874-1965

"It is easier to resist at the beginning than at the end."

-Leonardo di ser Piero da Vinci, 1452-1519

"Conscience warns us before it reproaches us."

-Comtesse Diane [Marie Josephine de Suin de Beausacq], 1829-1899

"From fanaticism to barbarianism is only one step."

-Denis Diderot, 1713-1784

"A man's most valuable trait is a judicious sense of what not to believe."

-Euripides, 485-406

"To have doubted one's own first principles is the mark of a civilized man."

-Oliver Wendell Holmes, Jun., 1841-1935

"Belief is not a form of knowledge but a free act, an expression of the will...it is for this reason that belief excludes all doubt."

-Søren Aabye Kierkegaard, 1813-1855

"There is a great difference between still believing something and believing it again."

-Georg Christoph Lichtenberg, 1742-1799

"With most men, unbelief in one thing springs from blind belief in another."

-Georg Christoph Lichtenberg, 1742-1799

"Conscience is the inner voice that warns us somebody may be looking."

-Henry Louis Mencken, 1880-1956

"The noblest people are the ones most troubled by conscience."

-Alan Oswald Moore, 1953-

"Few really believe. The most only believe that they believe or even make believe."

-Napoléon I [Napoléon Bonaparte], 1769-1821

"A very popular error—having the courage of one's convictions: Rather it is a matter of having the courage for an attack upon one's convictions."

-Friedrich Wilhelm Nietzsche, 1844-1900

"Belief in truth begins with doubting all that has hitherto been believed to be true."

-Friedrich Wilhelm Nietzsche, 1844-1900

"Convictions are more dangerous foes of truth than lies."

-Friedrich Wilhelm Nietzsche, 1844-1900

"Sometimes the best way to convince someone he is wrong is to let him have his way."

-Red O'Donnell, 1900-1984

"Few men make themselves masters of the things they write or speak."

-John Selden, 1564-1654

"If you would convince others, seem open to conviction yourself."

-Philip Dormer Stanhope, 4th Earl of Chesterfield, 1694-1773

"It is often easier to fight for one's principles than to live up to them."

-Adlai Ewing Stevenson II, 1900-1965

"It is to be believed because it is absurd."

-Quintus Septimus Tertullianus, c. 160-c. 240 B.C.

"That which has always been accepted by everyone, everywhere is almost certain to be false."

-Ambroise-Paul-Toussaint-Jules Valéry, 1871-1945

"It is almost impossible to state what one in fact believes, because it is almost impossible to hold a belief and to define it at the same time."

-Charles Walter Stansby Williams, 1886-1945

Bore(dom)

See also Interests

"Bore, *noun*. A person who talks when you wish him to listen."

-Ambrose Gwinnett Bierce, 1842-1914

"A yawn is a silent yell."

-Gilbert Keith Chesterton, 1874-1936

"We frequently forgive those who bore us, but cannot forgive those whom we bore."

-François VI, Duc de La Rochefoucauld, 1613-1680

"A bore is a man who deprives you of solitude without providing you with company."

-Giovanni Vincenzo Gravina, 1664-1718

"A variety of nothing is superior to a monotony of something."

-*Ascribed to* Johann Paul Friedrich Richter, 1763-1825

"The secret of being a bore is to tell everything."

-Voltaire [François Marie Arouet], 1694-1778

Business

"The price one pays for pursuing any profession or calling is an intimate knowledge of its ugly side."

-James Arthur Baldwin, 1924-1987

"An unfulfilled vocation drains the color from a man's entire existence."

-Honoré de Balzac, 1799-1850

"Whenever you see a successful business, someone once made a courageous decision."

-Peter Ferdinand Drucker, 1909-2005

"All professional men are handicapped by not being allowed to ignore things which are useless."

-Johann Wolfgang von Goethe, 1749-1834

"There is no kind of idleness by which we are so easily seduced as that which dignifies itself by the appearance of business."

-Dr. Samuel Johnson, 1709-1784

"Men in business are in as much danger from those at work under them as form those that work against them."

-George Savile, 1st Marquess of Halifax, 1633-1695

"Every man has business and desire."

-William Shakespeare, 1565-1616

"Perpetual devotion to what a man calls his business is only to be sustained by perpetual neglect of many other things."

-Robert Louis Balfour Stevenson, 1850-1894

"When two men in business always agree, one of them is unnecessary."

-William Wrigley, Jun., 1861-1932

Chance

See also: Luck, Opportunity, Success

"A throw of the dice will never abolish chance."

-Stéphane Mallarmé [Étienne Mallarmé], 1842-1898

"Chance favors the prepared mind."

-Louis Pasteur, 1822-1895

"Grab a chance and you won't be sorry for a might have been."

-Arthur Mitchell Ransome, 1884-1967

"He that leaveth nothing to Chance will do few things ill, but he will do very few things."

-George Savile, 1st Marquess of Halifax, 1633-1695

"Why not go out on a limb? Isn't that where the fruit is?"

-Frank Scully, 1892-1964

"Skating on thin ice is better than skating on no ice at all."

-John M. Shanahan, 1939-

"If you're never scared or embarrassed or hurt, it means you never take any chances."

-Julia Sorel [Rosalyn Drexler], 1926-

"Chance does nothing that has not been prepared beforehand."

-Alexis de Tocqueville, 1805-1859

Change

"Consider how hard it is to change yourself and you'll understand what little chance you have in trying to change others."

-Jacob Morton Braude

"You can't change for others, only for yourself."

-Brogan Lee Fullmer, 1988-

"You must be the change you wish to see in the world."

> -*Ascribed to* Mohandas Karamchand Gandhi, 1869-1948

"Everybody wants to be somebody: Nobody wants to grow."

> -Johann Wolfgang von Goethe, 1749-1834

"Tears will get you sympathy; sweat will get you change."

> -*Ascribed to* Jesse Louis Jackson, Sen., 1941-

"Be not angry that you cannot make others as you wish them to be, since you cannot make yourself as you wish to be."

> -Thomas à Kempis, 1380-1471

"Never doubt that a small group of thoughtful, committed citizens can change the world. Indeed, it's the only thing that ever has."

> -Margaret Mead, 1901-1978

"Some people change when they see the light, others when they feel the heat."

> -*Ascribed to* Caroline Schoeder

"Progress is impossible without change, and those who cannot change their minds cannot change anything."

> -George Bernard Shaw, 1856-1950

"Nothing is so painful to the human mind as a great and sudden change."

> -Mary Wollstonecraft Shelley, 1797-1851

"Before you can change someone else, you must change yourself."

> -Adam Sosne

"Everyone thinks of changing the world, but no one thinks of changing himself."

> -*Ascribed to* Lev Nikolayevich "Leo" Tolstoy, Comte Tolstoy, 1828-1910

"The most powerful agent of growth and transformation is something much more basic than any technique: a change of heart."

> -John Welwood

"If nothing ever changed there'd be no butterflies."

> -Anonymous

Chaos

"Chaos often breeds life, when order breeds habit."

-Henry Brooks Adams, 1838-1918

"We adore chaos because we love to produce order."

-Mauritis Cornelius Escher, 1898-1972

"If disorder is the rule with you, you will be penalized for installing order."

-Ambroise-Paul-Toussaint-Jules Valéry, 1871-1945

Character

See also: Attitude, Philosophy, Religion, Thought

"Resolve to be thyself; and know that he who finds himself loses his misery."

-Matthew Arnold, 1822-1888

"Up to a certain point every man is what he thinks he is."

-Francis Herbert Bradley, 1846-1924

"Character is what you know you are, not what others think you have."

-*Ascribed to* Marva Nettles Collins, 1936-

"The fault of every character comes from not listening."

-David Drake, 1945-

"People seem not to see that their opinion of the world is also a confession of character."

-Ralph Waldo Emerson, 1803-1882

"A talent is formed in stillness, a character in the world's torrent."

-*Ascribed to* Charles James Fox, 1749-1806

"Men show their character in nothing more clearly than by what they think laughable."

-Johann Wolfgang von Goethe, 1749-1834

"Of all cold words of tongue or pen, the worst are these: 'I knew him when—'"

-Arthur Guiterman, 1871-1943

"A man's character is his fate."

-Heraclitus, c. 540-c. 480 B.C.

"Almost every man wastes part of his life in attempts to display qualities which he does not possess, and to gain applause which he cannot keep."

-Dr. Samuel Johnson, 1709-1784

"It is through chance that, from among the various individuals of which each of us is composed, one emerges rather than another."

-Henry de Montherlant, 1896-1972

"You can tell the character of every man when you see how he receives praise."

-Lucius Annaeus Seneca, c. 4 B.C.-65

"People often say that this or that person has not yet found himself. But the self is not something one finds, it is something one creates."

-Thomas Stephen Szasz, 1920-

"Everyone is a moon, and has a dark side which he never shows to anybody."

-Mark Twain [Samuel Langhorne Clemens], 1835-1910

"Nothing is truer in a sense than a funeral oration: It tells precisely what the dead man should have been."

-*Ascribed to* Gustave Vapereau, 1909-1942

"Only the shallow know themselves."

-Oscar Fingal O'Flahertie Wilde, 1854-1900

Charity

See also Help, Love

"The way to feel better about our own situation is to improve someone else's circumstances."

-Ezra Taft Benson, 1899-1994

"Life's most persistent and urgent question is: What are you doing for others."

-Dr. Martin Luther King, Jun., 1929-1968

"Maturity begins to grow when you can sense your concern for others outweighing your concern for yourself."

-Ascribed to John Macnaughton

"Beggars should be abolished. It annoys one to give to them, and it annoys one not to give to them."

-Friedrich Wilhelm Nietzsche, 1844-1900

"One person caring about another represents life's greatest value."

-Ascribed to Jim Rohn

"What wisdom can you find that is greater than kindness?"

-Jean-Jacques Rousseau, 1712-1778

"People want condolences, not solutions."

-Ascribed to John Zacary "Zac" Spencer, 1989-

"He gives twice who gives promptly."

-Publilius Syrus, first century B.C.

"Candor and generosity, unless tempered by due moderation, lead to ruin."

-Cornelius Tacitus, 56-120

"If you pick up a starving dog and make him prosperous, he will not bite you. This is the principal difference between a dog and a man."

-Mark Twain [Samuel Langhorne Clemens], 1835-1910

"The man who leaves money to charity in his will is only giving away what no longer belongs to him."

-Voltaire [François Marie Arouet], 1694-1778

"You can give without loving, but you cannot love without giving."

-Richard Duane "Rick" Warren, 1954-

"All give some, some give all."

-Anonymous

Children

See also Age

"It is always self-defeating to pretend to the style of a generation younger than your own; it simply erases your own experience in history."

-Renata Adler, 1938-

"Children's talent to endure stems from their ignorance of alternatives."

-Maya Angelou [Marguerite Johnson], 1928-

"Children have never been good at listening to their elders, but they have never failed to imitate them."

-James Arthur Balwin, 1924-1987

"I am not young enough to know everything."

-Sir James Matthew Barrie, 1st Baronet of Adelphi Terrace, 1860-1937

"Young men think old men are fools; but old men know young men are fools."

-George Chapman, 1559-1634

"Every parent is at some time the father of the unreturned prodigal, with nothing to do but keep his house open to hope."

-John Anthony Ciardi, 1916-1986

"The most important thing that parents can teach their children is how to get along without them."

-Frank A. Clark, 1911-

"It is better to waste one's youth than to do nothing with it at all."

-*Ascribed to* Georges Courteline [Georges-Victor-Marcel Moineau], 1858-1929

"Almost everything that is great has been done by youth."

-Benjamin Disraeli, Earl of Beaconsfield, 1804-1881

"My best creation is my children."

-Diane von Fürstenberg, 1946-

"If one could recover the uncompromising spirit of one's youth, one's greatest indignation would be for what one has become."

-André Paul Guillaume Gide, 1869-1951

"Unlike grownups, children have little need to deceive themselves."

-*Ascribed to* Johann Wolfgang von Goethe, 1749-1834

"Children need models more than critics."

-Joseph Joubert, 1754-1824

"Oh what a tangled web do parents weave when they think that their children are naive."

-Frederic Ogden Nash, 1902-1971

"Children are the living messages we send to a time we will not see."

-Neil Postman, 1931-2003

"The young have aspirations that never come to pass, the old have reminiscences of what never happened."

-Saki [Hector Hugh Monro], 1870-1916

"A baby is God's opinion that life should go on."

-Carl August Sandburg, 1878-1967

"The deepest definition of youth is life as yet untouched by tragedy."

-Alfred North Whitehead, 1861-1947

"Don't limit a child to your own learning, for he was born in another time."

-Anonymous

Confidence

See also: Beliefs, Faith, Respect, Trust

"We rarely confide in those who are better than we are."

-Albert Camus, 1913-1960

"No one who deserves confidence ever solicits it."

-John Churton Collins, 1848-1908

"The more you like yourself, the less you are like anyone else, which makes you unique."

-*Ascribed to* Walter Elias Disney, 1901-1966

"For a man to achieve all that is demanded of him he must regard himself as greater than he is."

-*Ascribed to* Johann Wolfgang von Goethe, 1749-1834

"We have to serve our self many years before we gain our own confidence."

-*Ascribed to* Henry Samuel Haskins, 1878-1957

"Self-respect is the root of discipline: The sense of dignity grows with the ability to say no to oneself."

-Abraham Joshua Heschel, 1907-1972

"He that respects himself is safe from others; he wears a coat of mail that none can pierce."

-Henry Wadsworth Longfellow, 1807-1882

"Confidence comes not from always being right but from not fearing to be wrong."

-*Ascribed to* Peter T. McIntyre

"No one can make you feel inferior without your consent."

-Anna Eleanor Roosevelt, 1884-1962

"Every man has to seek in his own way to make his own self more noble and to realize his own true worth."

-Ascribed to Dr. Albert Schweitzer, 1875-1965

"Authority must come from above, confidence from below."

-Emmanuel Joseph Sieyès, 1748-1836

Conflict

See also: Enemies, Peace, War

"Violence is the last refuge of the incompetent."

-Isaac Asimov, 1920-1992

"Nothing in the world is so exhilarating as to be shot at without result."

-Ascribed to Sir Winston Leonard Spencer Churchill, 1874-1965

"Quarrels would not last long if the fault were only on one side."

-François VI, Duc de La Rochefoucauld, 1613-1680

"Never contend with a man who has nothing to lose."

-Baltasar Gracián, 1601-1658

"Silence is argument carried on by other means."

-Ascribed to Ernesto "Che" Guevara, 1928-1967

"I have found you an argument; I am not obliged to find you an understanding."

-Dr. Samuel Johnson, 1709-1784

"You raise your voice when you should reinforce your argument."

-Ascribed to Dr. Samuel Johnson, 1709-1784

"Violence and injury enclose in their net all that do such things, and general return upon him who began."

-Lucretius [Tirus Lucretius Carus], c. 99- c. 55 B.C.

"Who overcomes by force hath overcome but half his foe."

-John Milton, 1608-1674

"What does not destroy me makes me stronger."

-Friedrich Wilhelm Nietzsche, 1844-1900

"The most savage controversies are those about matters as to which there is no good evidence either way."

-Bertrand Arthur William Russell, 3rd Earl of Russell, 1872-1970

"Beware of entrance to a quarrel, but, being in, bear't that th' opposed may beware of thee."

-William Shakespeare, 1564-1616

"Were it my cue to fight, I should have known it without a prompter."

-William Shakespeare, 1564-1616

"Assassination is the extreme form of censorship."

-George Bernard Shaw, 1856-1950

"The test of a man or woman's breeding is how they behave in a quarrel."

-George Bernard Shaw, 1856-1950

"In quarreling, the truth is always lost."

-Publilius Syrus, first century B.C.

"A hurtful act is the transference to others of the degradation which we bear in ourselves."

-Simone Weil, 1909-1943

"Violence is, essentially, a confession of ultimate inarticulateness."

-*Time*

Courage

"Until the day of his death, no man can be sure of his courage."

-Jean Anouilh, 1910-1987

"Courage is fear that has said its prayers."

-*Ascribed to* Karl Barth, 1886-1968

"Courage is rightly esteemed the first of human qualities because...it is the quality which guarantees all others."

-Sir Winston Leonard Spencer Churchill, 1874-1965

"Courage is the quality most essential to understanding the language of the world."

-Paulo Coelho, 1947-

"That all men would be cowards if they dare,
Some men we know have courage to declare;
And this the life of many an hero shows,
That like the tide, man's courage ebbs and flows"

-George Crabbe, 1754-1832

"A great part of courage is the courage of having done the thing before."

-Ralph Waldo Emerson, 1803-1882

"Perfect courage means doing unwitnessed what we would be capable of with the world looking on."

-François VI, Duc de La Rochefoucauld, 1613-1680

"Many would be cowards if they had courage enough."

-Dr. Thomas Fuller, 1654-1734

"Some have been thought brave because they were afraid to run away."

-Dr. Thomas Fuller, 1654-1734

"One man with courage makes a majority."

-*Ascribed* to Andrew Jackson, 1767-1845

"Dare to do things worthy of imprisonment if you mean to be of consequence."

-Juvenal [Decimus Junius Juvenalis], 55-130

"One never dives into the water to save a drowning man more eagerly than when there are others present who dare not take the risk."

-Friedrich Wilhelm Nietzsche, 1844-1900

"Life shrinks or expands in proportion to one's courage."

-Anaïs Nin, 1903-1977

"Courage is fear holding on a minute longer."

-George Smith Patton, Jun., 1885-1945

"Courage is doing what you're afraid to do. There can be no courage unless you're scared."

-Edward Vernon Rickenbacker, 1890-1973

"Conscience doth make cowards of us all."

-William Shakespeare, 1565-1616

"The test of courage comes when we are in the minority: the test of tolerance comes when we are in the majority."

-Ralph Washington Sockman, 1889-1970

"Courage is resistance to fear, mastery of fear, not absence of fear."

-Mark Twain [Samuel Langhorne Clemens], 1835-1910

"Except a person be part coward, it is not a compliment to say he is brave."

-Mark Twain [Samuel Langhorne Clemens], 1835-1910

"Courage is the art of being the only one who knows you're scared to death."

-James Harold Wilson, Baron of Rievaulx, 1916-1995

"Many become brave when brought to bay."

-Norwegian proverb

"As cowardly as a coward is, it is not safe to call a coward a coward."

-Anonymous

Creativity

"Be brave enough to live life creatively. The creative is the place where no one else has ever been."

-Alan Alda [Alfonso Joseph D'Abruzzo], 1936-

"In any evolutionary process, even in the arts, the search for novelty becomes corrupting."

-Kenneth Ewart Boulding, 1910-1993

"Creativity is inventing, experimenting, growing, taking risks, breaking rules, making mistakes, and having fun."

-Dr. Mary Lou Cook

"Of the truly creative no one is ever master; it must be left to go its own way."

-*Ascribed to* Johann Wolfgang von Goethe, 1749-1834

"What is originality? Undetected plagiarism."

-William Ralph Inge, 1860-1954

"The creative mind plays with the objects it loves."

-Carl Gustav Jung, 1875-1961

"In creating, the only hard thing's to begin; a grass-blade's no easier to make than an oak."

-James Russell Lowell, 1819-1891

"Creativity is the power to connect the seemingly unconnected."

-Sir William Palmer, 1803-1885

"The more intelligent a man is, the more originality he discovers in men. Ordinary people see no difference between men."

-Blaise Pascal, 1623-1662

"Originality consists in thinking for yourself, not in thinking differently from other people."

-Sir James Fitzjames Stephen, 1st Baronet Stephen, 1829-1894

"One of your most powerful inner resources is your own creativity."

-*Ascribed to* Marcia Wieder

"Consistency is the last refuge of the unimaginative."

-Oscar Fingal O'Flahertie Wilde, 1854-1900

"A good spectator also creates."

-Swiss proverb

"He who is most creative conceals his sources the best."

-Anonymous

"Necessity is the mother of all invention."

-Anonymous

Crime

See also Evil, Sin

"Crime expands according to our willingness to put up with it."

-Barry Farber, 1947-

"If poverty is the mother of all crimes, lack of intelligence is their father."

-Jean de La Bruyère, 1645-1695

"The criminal element now calculates that crime really does pay."

-Ronald Wilson Reagan, 1911-2004

"Crime is a logical extension of the sort of behavior that is often considered perfectly respectable in legitimate business."

-Robert Rice, 1916-?

"Men are not hanged for stealing horses, but that horses may not be stolen."

-George Savile, 1st Marquess of Halifax, 1633-1695

"A criminal is a person which predatory instincts who has not sufficient capital to form a corporation."

-*Ascribed to* Howard Scott, 1926-?

Criticism

See also Praise, Respect

"The course of a river is almost always disapproved of by its source."

-Jean Maurice Eugène Clément Cocteau, 1889-1963

"Those not present are always wrong."

-Philippe Néricault Destouches, 1680-1754

"You know who the critics are? The men who have failed in literature and art."

-Benjamin Disraeli, Earl of Beaconsfield, 1804-1881

"We resent all criticism which denies us anything that lies in our line of advance."

-Ralph Waldo Emerson, 1803-1882

"One becomes a critic when one cannot be an artist, just as a man becomes a stool pigeon when he cannot be a soldier."

-Gustave Flaubert, 1821-1880

"Against criticism a man can neither protest nor defend himself; he must act in spite of it, and then it will gradually yield to him."

-Johann Wolfgang von Goethe, 1749-1834

"To escape criticism: Do nothing, say nothing, be nothing."

-Elbert Green Hubbard, 1856-1915

"Nothing will ever be attempted, if all possible objections must be first overcome."

-Dr. Samuel Johnson, 1709-1784

"Never speak ill of yourself, your friends will always say enough on that subject."

-Charles Maurice, Comte de Talleyrand-Périgord, 1754-1838

"Criticism itself is no more than prejudice made plausible."

-Henry Louis Mencken, 1880-1956

"No matter how well you perform there's always somebody of intelligent opinion who thinks it's lousy."

-*Ascribed to* Laurence Kerr Olivier, Baron Olivier, 1907-1989

"Look for the ridiculous in everything, and you will find it."

-Jules Renard, 1864-1910

"Ridicule often checks what is absurd, and fully as often smothers that which is noble."

-Sir Walter Scott, 1771-1832

"Silence is the most perfect expression of scorn."

-George Bernard Shaw, 1856-1950

"An injury is much sooner forgotten than an insult."

-Philip Dormer Stanhope, 4th Earl of Chesterfield, 1694-1773

"To show resentment at a reproach is to acknowledge that one may have deserved it."

-Cornelius Tacitus, 56-120

"He only may chastise who loves."

-Rabindranath Tagore, 1861-1941

"You must not pay a person a compliment, and then straightway follow it with criticism."

-Mark Twain [Samuel Langhorne Clemens], 1835-1910

"Two and two the mathematician continues to make four, in spite of the whine of the amateur for three, or the cry of the critic for five."

-James McNeill Whistler, 1834-1903

"There is luxury in self-reproach. When we blame ourselves, we feel no one else has a right to blame us."

-Oscar Fingal O'Flahertie Wilde, 1854-1900

Death

See also Life

"As a well-spent day brings happy sleep, so a life well used brings happy death."

-Leonardo di ser Piero da Vinci, 1452-1519

"The graveyards are full of indispensable men."

-*Ascribed to* Charles André Joseph Marie de Gaulle, 1890-1970

"Any man's death diminishes me, because I am involved in mankind; and therefore never send to know for whom the bell tolls; it tolls for thee."

-John Donne, 1572-1631

"One short sleep past, we wake eternally, and death shall be no more; death, thou shalt die."

-John Donne, 1572-1631

"I cannot help being more frightened at the idea of malediction of the dead than the hatred of the living."

-Alexandre Dumas, Père [Dumas Davy de la Pailleterie], 1802-1870

"Death is nothing to us, since when we are, death has not come, and when death has come, we are not."

-Epicurus, c. 341-270 B.C.

"All the arts and sciences have their roots in the struggle against death."

-*Ascribed to* Saint Gregory of Nyssa, 335-394

"Our repugnance to death increases in proportion to our consciousness of having lived in vain."

-William Hazlitt, 1778-1830

"Pale death with impartial tread beats at the poor man's cottage door and at the palaces of kings."

-Horace [Quintus Horatius Flaccus], 65-8 B.C.

"There is not, perhaps, to a mind well instructed, a more painful occurrence, than the death of one we have injured without reparation."

-Dr. Samuel Johnson, 1709-1784

"By protracting life, we do not deduct one jot from the duration of death."

-Lucretius [Tirus Lucretius Carus], c. 99- c. 55 B.C.

"Death is a distant rumor to the young."

-Andrew Aitken Rooney, 1919-2011

"Kill a man, and you are a murderer. Kill millions of men, and you are a conqueror. Kill everyone and you are a god."

-Jean Rostand, 1894-1977

"After your death you will be what you were before your birth."

-Arthur Schopenhauer, 1788-1860

"To examine the causes of life, we must first recourse to death."

-Mary Wollstonecraft Shelley, 1797-1851

"The fear of death is more to be dreaded than death itself."

-Publilius Syrus, first century B.C.

"Death twitches my ear. 'Live,' he says, 'I am coming.'"

-Virgil [Publius Vergilius Maro], 70-19 B.C.

"Now I become death, the destroyer of worlds."

-The *Bhagavad Gita* 11:32

Deception

See also: Honesty, Lies, Truth, Trust

"We discover in ourselves what others hide from us, and we recognize in others what we hide from ourselves."

-Luc de Clapiers, Marquis de Vauvenargues, 1715-1747

"Never believe anything until it has been officially denied."

-Francis Claud Cockburn, 1904-1981

"Nothing is easier than self-deceit. For what each man wishes, that he also believes to be true."

-Demosthenes, 384-322

"All falsehood is a mask which however well fashioned, reveals its shams upon close inspection."

-Alexandre Dumas, Père [Dumas Davy de la Pailleterie], 1802-1870

"It is impossible for a man to be cheated by anyone but himself."

-Ralph Waldo Emerson, 1803-1882

"The true way to be deceived is to think oneself more clever than others."

-François VI, Duc de La Rochefoucauld, 1613-1680

"It is better to be deceived by one's friends than to deceive them."

-Johann Wolfgang von Goethe, 1749-1834

"Anyone who can handle a needle convincingly can make us see a thread which is not there."

-Sir Ernst Hans Josef Gombrich, 1909-2001

"Our greatest pretenses are built up not to hide the evil and the ugly in us, but our emptiness. The hardest thing to hide is something that is not there."

-Eric Hoffer, 1902-1983

"One's own self is well hidden form one's own self; of all mines of treasure, one's own is the last to be dug up."

-Friedrich Wilhelm Nietzsche, 1844-1900

"Everything that deceives may be said to enchant."

-Plato, c. 428-348

"Who are next to knaves? Those that converse with them."

-Alexander Pope, 1688-1744

"A little inaccuracy saves tons of explanation."

-Saki [Hector Hugh Monro], 1870-1916

"Things are entirely what they appear to be and behind them...there is nothing."

-Jean-Paul Charles Aymard Sartre, 1905-1980

"Oh, what a tangled web we weave,
When first we practice to deceive!"

-Sir Walter Scott, 1771-1832

"Distrust all those who love you extremely upon a very slight acquaintance and without any visible reason."

-Philip Dormer Stanhope, 4th Earl of Chesterfield, 1694-1773

"There is a demand today for men who can make wrong appear right."

-*Ascribed to* Terence [Publius Terentius Afer], c. 190- c. 159 B.C.

"He who fondles you more than usual has either deceived you or wants to do so."

-French proverb

"Crafty men deal in generalizations."

-Anonymous

Decisions

See also Beliefs, Judgment

"Endurance is frequently a form of indecision."

-Elizabeth Bibesco, 1897-1945

"One-half of the troubles of this life can be traced to saying yes too quickly and not saying no soon enough."

-Josh Billings [Henry Wheeler Shaw], 1818-1885

"A committee is a cul-de-sac down which ideas are lured and then quickly strangled."

-*Ascribed to* Sir Barnett Cocks, 1907-1989

"Chi Wen Tzu always thought three times before taking action. Twice would have been quite enough."

-Confucius, c. 551-479 B.C.

"Soon after a hard decision, something inevitably occurs to cast doubt. Holding steady against that doubt usually proves the decision."

-Robert Irvine Fitzhenry, 1918-2008

"The most decisive actions of our life...are most often unconsidered actions."

-André Paul Guillaume Gide, 1869-1951

"If Columbus had an advisory committee he would probably still be at the dock."

-*Ascribed to* Arthur Joseph Goldberg, 1908-1990

"What is a committee? A group of the unwilling, picked from the unfit, to do the unnecessary."

-Richard Long Harkness, 1907-1977

"The buyer needs a hundred eyes, the seller not one."

-George Herbert, 1593-1633

"Take time to deliberate; but when the time for action arrives, stop thinking and go in."

-Andrew Jackson, 1767-1845

"And the trouble is, if you don't risk anything, you risk even more."

-Erica Jong, 1942-

"During the first period of a man's life the greatest danger is not to take the risk."

-Søren Aabye Kierkegaard, 1813-1855

"It seems more practical to go directly to the actual truth of the matter than to speculate about it."

-Niccolò Machiavelli, 1469-1527

"If someone tells you he is going to make 'a realistic decision,' you immediately understand that he has resolved to do something bad."

-Mary Therese McCarthy, 1912-1989

"Decide promptly, but never give any reasons. Your decisions may be right, but your reasons are sure to be wrong."

-William Murray, 1st Earl of Mansfield, 1705-1793

"Living movements do not come of committees."

-John Henry Newman, Cardinal-Deacon San Giorgio al Velabro, 1801-1890

"Executive ability—deciding quickly and getting somebody else to do the work."

-John Garland Pollard, 1871-1937

"The essence of strategy is choosing what not to do."

-Michael Eugene Porter, 1947-

"All our final resolutions are made in a state of mind which is not going to last."

-Valentin Louis Georges Eugène Marcel Proust, 1871-1922

"A decision is the action an executive must take when he has information so incomplete that the answer does not suggest itself."

-Arthur William Radford, 1896-1973

"A committee of one gets things done."

-Joe Ryan, 1951-

"Never tell your resolution beforehand."

-John Selden, 1584-1654

"If you take too long in deciding what to do with your life, you'll find you've done it."

-George Bernard Shaw, 1856-1950

"In the choice of a horse and a wife, a man must please himself, ignoring the opinion and advice of friends."

-George John Whyte-Melville, 1821-1878

Desires

See also: Ambition, Dreams, Goals

"All men are tempted. There is no man that lives that can't be broken down, provided it is the right temptation, put in the right spot."

-Henry Ward Beecher, 1813-1887

"We grow weary of those things (and perhaps soonest) which we most desire."

-Samuel Butler, 1612-1680

42

"Men's passions are so many roads by which they can be reached."

-*Ascribed to* Luc de Clapiers, Marquess de Vauvenargues, 1715-1747

"You must always know what it is that you want."

-Paulo Coelho, 1947-

"The man who is master of his passions is Reason's slave."

-Cyril Vernon Connolly, 1903-1974

"The formula 'two and two make five' is not without its attractions."

-Fyodor Mikhailovich Dostoevsky, 1821-1881

"Nothing is so good as it seems beforehand."

-George Eliot [Marian Evans Cross], 1819-1880

"Necessity never made a good bargain."

-Dr. Benjamin Franklin, 1706-1790

"The true use of speech is not so much to express our wants as to conceal them."

-Oliver Goldsmith, 1728-1774

"He that has satisfied his thirst turns his back on the well."

-Baltasar Gracián, 1601-1658

"I have not been afraid of excess: Excess on occasion is exhilarating. It prevents moderation from acquiring the deadening effect of a habit."

-William Somerset Maugham, 1874-1965

"One of the oldest human needs is having someone to wonder where you are when you don't come home at night."

-Margaret Mead, 1901-1978

"If you give a mouse a cookie, he's going to want a glass of milk."

-Laura Joffe Numeroff, 1953-

"We do not do what we want and yet we are responsible for what we are-that is the fact."

-Jean-Paul Charles Aymard Sartre, 1905-1980

"Things sweet the taste prove in digestion sour."

-William Shakespeare, 1564-1616

"Life contains but two tragedies. One is not to get your heart's desire; the other is to get it."

-George Bernard Shaw, 1856-1950

"'Tis not the meat, but 'tis the appetite makes eating a delight."

-Sir John Suckling, 1609-1642

"In this world there are only two tragedies. One is not getting what one wants, and the other is getting it."

-Oscar Fingal O'Flahertie Wilde, 1854-1900

"The only way to get rid of a temptation is to yield to it."

-Oscar Fingal O'Flahertie Wilde, 1854-1900

"Hope deferred maketh the heart sick: but when the desire cometh it is a tree of life."

-*The Proverbs* 13:12

"If the camel once gets his nose in a tent, his body will soon follow."

-Saudi Arabian proverb

Destiny

See also Future, History

"Whatso'er we perpetrate,
We do but row; we are steered by fate."

-Samuel Butler, 1612-1680

"I do not believe in a fate that falls on men however they act; but I do not believe in a fate that falls on men unless they act."

-Gilbert Keith Chesterton, 1874-1936

"The efforts which we make to escape from our destiny only serve to lead us into it."

-Ralph Waldo Emerson, 1803-1882

"Wherever a man may happen to turn, whatever a man may undertake, he will always end up by returning to that path which nature has marked out for him."

-Johann Wolfgang von Goethe, 1749-1834

"You had better be a round peg in a square hole than a square peg in a square hole. The latter is in for life, while the first is only an indeterminate sentence."

-Elbert Green Hubbard, 1856-1915

"There's a divinity that shapes our ends, rough-hew them how we will—"

-William Shakespeare, 1564-1616

"Who can control his fate?"

-William Shakespeare, 1564-1616

"Control your own destiny or someone will else will."

-John Francis "Jack" Welch, Jun., 1935-

"Fate goes as Fate must!"

-*Beowulf*

Determination

See also Strength

"A great flame follows a little spark."

-Dante Alighieri, 1265-1321

"If you would attain to what you are not yet, you must always be displeased by what you are. For where you are pleased with yourself there you have remained. Keep adding, keep walking, keep advancing."

-*Ascribed to* Saint Augustine [Aurelius Augustinus], 354-430

"Never give in. Never give in. Never, never, never, never—in nothing, great or small, large or petty—never give in, except to convictions of honor and good sense. Never yield to force. Never yield to the apparently overwhelming might of the enemy."

-Sir Winston Leonard Spencer Churchill, 1874-1965

"Determination and perseverance move the world; thinking that others will do it for you is a sure way to fail."

-Marva Nettles Collins, 1936-

"The fire which seems extinguished often slumbers beneath the ashes."

-Pierre Corneille, 1606-1684

"No steam or gas ever drives anything until it is confined. No Niagara is ever turned into light and power until it is tunneled. No life ever grows great until it is focused, dedicated, disciplined."

-Dr. Henry Emerson "Harry" Fosdick, 1878-1969

"Nothing is easy to the unwilling."

-Dr. Thomas Fuller, 1654-1734

"A determined soul will do more with a rusty monkey wrench than a loafer accomplish with all the tools in a machine shop."

-*Ascribed to* Robert Studley Forrest Hughes, 1938-2012

"The word impossible is not in my dictionary."

-*Ascribed to* Napoléon I [Napoléon Bonaparte], 1769-1821

"Victory belongs to the most preserving."

-*Ascribed to* Napoléon I [Napoléon Bonaparte], 1769-1821

"Even the hard-way is still a way."

-John Palmer

"An object in possession seldom retains the same charm that it had in pursuit."

-Pliny the Younger [Gaius Plinius Caecilius Secundis], c. 61-c. 112 B.C.

"Idleness is only the refuge of weak minds."

-Philip Dormer Stanhope, 4th Earl of Chesterfield, 1694-1773

Doubts

See also: Attitude, Beliefs, Philosophy, Religion, Thought

"To think is to say *no*."

-Émile-Auguste Chartier, 1868-1951

"To give a reason for anything is to breed a doubt of it."

-William Hazlitt, 1778-1830

"Skepticism is the chastity of the intellect, and it is shameful to surrender it too soon or to the first comer."

-George Santayana, 1863-1952

"A wise man will keep his suspicions muzzled, but he will keep them awake."

-George Savile, 1st Marquess of Halifax, 1633-1695

"Our doubts are traitors, and make us lose the good we oft might win, by fearing to attempt."

-William Shakespeare, 1564-1616

"The only interesting answers are those which destroy the questions."

-Susan Sontag, 1933-2004

"A proof tells us where to concentrate our doubts."

-Anonymous

Dreams

See also: Ambition, Desires, Ideas, Goals

"How swiftly our dreams soar on the wings of imagination!"

-Alexandre Dumas, Père [Dumas Davy de la Pailleterie], 1802-1870

"His dreams mocked to death by Time. That is the life of man."

-Zora Neale Hurston, 1891-1960

"Ships at a distance have every man's wish on board."

-Zora Neale Hurston, 1891-1960

"Vision is the art of seeing things invisible."

-Jonathan Swift, 1667-1745

"If you can imagine it, you can achieve it. If you can dream it, you can become it."

-William Arthur Ward, 1921-1994

"Like our shadows, our wishes lengthen as our sun declines."

-Edward Young, 1683-1765

"If you don't practice you don't deserve to dream"

-Anonymous

Education

See also: Genius, Intelligence, Knowledge, Teaching, Wisdom

"The investigation of the meaning of words is the beginning of education."

-Antisthenes, c. 445- c. 365 B.C.

"Educated men are as much superior to uneducated men as the living are to the dead."

-Aristotle, 384-322 B.C.

"Education is learning what you didn't even know you didn't know."

-Daniel Joseph Boorstin, 1914-2004

"Education makes people easy to lead, but difficult to drive; easy to govern but impossible to enslave."

-Henry Peter Brougham, 1st Baron Brougham and Vaux, 1778-1868

"Without education, we are in a horrible and deadly danger of taking educated people seriously."

-Gilbert Keith Chesterton, 1874-1936

"There is a brilliant child locked inside every student."

-Marva Nettles Collins, 1936-

"Learn as much by writing as by reading."

-John Emerich Edward Dalberg, 1st Baron Acton, 1834-1902

"There are the learners and the learned. Memory makes the one, philosophy the other."

-Alexandre Dumas, Père [Dumas Davy de la Pailleterie], 1802-1870

"Education is for improving the lives of others and for leaving your community and world better than you found it."

-Marian Wright Edelman, 1939-

"How we hate this solemn Ego that accompanies the learned, like a double, wherever he goes."

-Ralph Waldo Emerson, 1803-1882

"Who so neglects learning in his youth, loses the past and is dead for the future."

-Euripides, c. 485-406 B.C.

"The best-educated human being is the one who understands most about the life in which he is placed."

-Helen Adams Keller, 1880-1968

"A great deal of learning can be packed into an empty head."

-Karl Kraus, 1874-1936

"The more scholastically educated a man is generally, the more he is an emotional boor."

-David Herbert Lawrence, 1885-1930

"If you educate a man you educate a person, but if you educate a woman you educate a family."

-Ruby Manikan

"Let early education be a sort of amusement; you will then be better able to find out the natural bent."

-Plato, c. 428-c.348 B.C.

"We receive three different or contrary educations, one from our parents, one from our schoolmasters, and one from the world. The third contradicts all that the first two teach us."

-Charles-Louis de Secondat, Baron de La Brède et de Montesquieu, 1689-1750

"A mind of moderate capacity, which closely pursues one study, must infallibly arrive at great proficiency in that study."

-Mary Wollstonecraft Shelley, 1797-1851

Effort

See also Work

"Well begun is half done."

-Aristotle, 384-322

"Action springs not from thought, but from a read message for responsibility."

-Dietrich Bonhoeffer, 1906-1945

"A man who has to be convinced to act before he acts is not a man of action....You must act as you breathe."

-Georges Benjamin Clemenceau, 1841-1929

"The distance doesn't matter; it is only the first step that is difficult."

-Madame du Deffand [Marie de Vichy-Chamrond], Marquise de Deffand, 1697-1780

"God abandons those who abandon themselves."

-Alexandre Dumas, Père [Dumas Davy de la Pailleterie], 1802-1870

"Duty, then, is the sublimest word in our language....You cannot do more, you should never wish to do less."

-Robert Edward Lee, 1807-1870

"We never do anything well till we cease to think about the manner of doing it."

-William Hazlitt, 1778-1830

"Never mistake motion for action."

-Ernest Miller Hemingway, 1899-1961

"He who has begun has half done. Dare to be wise; begin!"

-Horace [Quintus Horatius Flaccus], 65-8 B.C

"Welcome the task that makes you go beyond yourself."

-Ascribed to Frank McGee, 1915-1974

"It's not so much how busy you are, but why you are busy. The bee is praised. The mosquito is swatted."

-Ascribed to Mary O'Connor

"When you pick up one end of the stick, you pick up the other as well."

-Boyd Kenneth Packer, 1924-

"Better never than late."

-George Bernard Shaw, 1856-1950

"You don't hold your own in the world by standing on guard, but by attacking and getting well hammered yourself."

-George Bernard Shaw, 1856-1950

"No matter how big or soft or warm your bed is, you still have to get out of it."

-Ascribed to Grace Barnett Slick, 1939-

"Nothing is impossible for the man who doesn't have to do it himself."

-Abraham H. "Abe" Weiler, 1908-2001

"Make voyages!—Attempt them! There's nothing else."

-Tennessee Williams [Thomas Lanier Williams III], 1911-1983

"If we don't try, then we don't do; and if we don't do, then why are we here?"

-From the Motion Picture *Shenandoah*, 1965

"If you wish to drown, do not torture yourself with shallow water."

-Bulgarian proverb

"He who is outside his door already has the hard part of his journey behind him."

-Dutch proverb

51

Enemies

See also Friends

"The haft of the arrow had been feathered with one of the eagle's own plumes. We often give our enemies the means of our own destruction."

-Aesop, c. 620- c. 550 B.C.

"He who has a thousand friends has not a friend to spare, and he who has one enemy will meet him everywhere."

-Ali ibn Abi-Talib, 602-661

"Pay attention to your enemies, for they are the first to discover your mistakes."

-Ascribed to Antisthenes, c. 445- c. 365 B.C.

"Better make a weak man your enemy than your friend."

-Josh Billings [Henry Wheeler Shaw], 1818-1885

"He that wrestles with us strengthens our nerves, and sharpens our skill. Our antagonist is our helper."

-Edmund Burke, 1729-1797

"Verily, the heart of the kindest of women is pitiless toward the misery of a rival."

-Alexandre Dumas, Père [Dumas Davy de la Pailleterie], 1802-1870

"There is no little enemy."

-Dr. Benjamin Franklin, 1706-1790

"A man with a career can have no time to waste upon his wife and friends—he has to devote it wholly to his enemies!"

-John Oliver Hobbes [Pearl Mary Teresa Craigie], 1867-1965

"You can discover what your enemy fears most by observing the means he uses to frighten you."

-Eric Hoffer, 1902-1983

"*Friend* is sometimes a word devoid of meaning; enemy, never."

-Victor Marie Hugo, 1802-1885

"Such seems to be the disposition of man, that whatever makes a distinction produces rivalry."

-Dr. Samuel Johnson, 1709-1784

"Our years, our debts, and our enemies are always more numerous than we imagine."

-Charles Nodier, 1780-1844

"To have a good enemy, choose a friend: He knows where to strike."

-Diane de Poitiers, Duchess de Valentinois, 1499-1566

"Whoever has his foe at his mercy, and does not kill him, is his own enemy."

-Sa'di [Musharrif-uddin], 1184-1291

"Be extremely subtle, to the point of formlessness. Be extremely mysterious, to the point of soundlessness. Thereby you can be the director of the opponent's fate."

-Sun-tzu, c. 544-496 B.C.

"It takes your enemy and your friend, working together, to hurt you to the heart; the one to slander you and the other to get the news to you."

-Mark Twain [Samuel Langhorne Clemens], 1835-1910

"A man cannot be too careful in the choice of his enemies."

-Oscar Fingal O'Flahertie Wilde, 1854-1900

"He that is not with me is against me; and he that gathereth not with me scattereth abroad."

-*The Gospel According to Matthew* 12:30

"The fire you kindle for your enemy often burns you more than him."

-Chinese proverb

"Beware the foe bringing gifts."

-Latin proverb

Equality

"Equality is the result of human organization. We are not born equal."

-Hannah Arendt, 1906-1975

"Inferiors revolt in order that they may be equal, and equals that they may be superior. Such is the state of mind which creates revolutions."

-Aristotle, 384-322 B.C.

"No snob welcomes another who has risen with him."

-Sir Cecil Walter Hardy Beaton, 1904-1980

"The woman who thinks she is intelligent demands equal rights with men. A woman who is intelligent does not."

-*Ascribed to* Sidonie-Gabrielle Colette, 1873-1954

"Equality is what does not exist among equals."

-Edward Estlin Cummings, 1894-1962

"Men are made by nature unequal. It is vain, therefore, to treat them as if they were equal."

-James Anthony Froude, 1818-1894

"That all men are equal is a proposition to which, at ordinary times, no sane individual has ever given his assent."

-Aldous Leonard Huxley, 1894-1963

"All men are equal before god. Wisdom, talents, and virtue, are the only difference between them."

-Napoléon I [Napoléon Bonaparte], 1769-1821

"All animals are equal, but some animals are more equal than others."

-George Orwell [Eric Blair], 1903-1950

"Humanity is composed but of two categories, the invalids and the nurses."

-Richard Brinsley Sheridan, 1751-1816

Evil

See also: Good, Morality, Sin, Vice, Virtue

"The belief in a supernatural source of evil is not necessary; men alone are quite capable of every wickedness."

-Joseph Conrad, 1857-1924

"The most beautiful face may conceal the most evil of hearts."

-Alexandre Dumas, Père [Dumas Davy de la Pailleterie], 1802-1870

"Evil deeds do not prosper; the slow man catches up with the swift."

-Homer, 700 B.C

"In order to do good, you may have to engage in evil."

-Robert Strange McNamara, 1916-2009

"For neither man nor angel can discern hypocrisy, the only evil that walks invisible."

-John Milton, 1608-1674

"The test of what is evil is not its degree, but its effect."

-Dallin Harris Oaks, 1932-

"You cannot have power for good without having power for evil too. Even mother's milk nourishes murderers as well as heroes."

-George Bernard Shaw, 1856-1950

"You are permitted in time of great danger to walk with the devil until you have crossed the bridge."

-Bulgarian proverb

"The darkest hour of the night comes just before dawn."

-English proverb

"The devil's boots don't creak."

-Scottish proverb

Experience

See also: Education, Intelligence, Judgment, Knowledge, Teaching

"Experience is a good teacher, but she sends in terrific bills."

-Minna Antrim, 1856-1950

"To a great experience one thing is essential, an experiencing nature. It is not enough to have opportunity; it is essential to feel it."

-Walter Bagehot, 1826-1877

"Experience does not err; it is only your judgment that errs in expecting from her what is not in her power."

-Leonardo di ser Piero da Vinci, 1452-1519

"Experience is not what happens to a man. It is what a man does with what happens to him."

-Aldous Leonard Huxley, 1894-1963

"Everyone is perfectly willing to learn from unpleasant experience—if only the damage of the first lesson could be repaired."

-Georg Christoph Lichtenberg, 1742-1799

"It's not what happens to you in life, it's what you do about it."

-W. Mitchell [William John Schiff III], 1943-

"Experience is the name everyone gives to his mistakes."

-Oscar Fingal O'Flahertie Wilde, 1854-1900

"I like men who have a future and women who have a past."

-Oscar Fingal O'Flahertie Wilde, 1854-1900

"Experience is what you get when you didn't get what you wanted."

-Italian proverb

"The trouble with using experiences as a guide is that the final exam often comes first and then the lesson."

-Anonymous

Failure

See also: (Mis)Fortune, Luck, Success

"Nothing fails like success because we don't learn from it. We learn only from failure."

-Kenneth Ewart Boulding, 1910-1993

"All men that are ruined are ruined on the side of their natural propensities."

-Edmund Burke, 1729-1797

"The first undertakers in all great attempts commonly miscarry, and leave the advantages of their losses to those that come after them."

-Samuel Butler, 1612-1680

"Failure is only the opportunity to begin more intelligently."

-Henry Ford, 1863-1947

"If a man once falls, all will tread upon him."

-Dr. Thomas Fuller, 1654-1734

"Fish die belly-upward and rise to the surface; it is their way of falling."

-André Paul Guillaume Gide, 1869-1951

"It is often the failure who is the pioneer in new lands, new undertakings, and new forms of expression."

-Eric Hoffer, 1902-1983

"Failure is not the only punishment for laziness; there is also the success of others."

-Jules Renard, 1864-1910

"You always pass failure on your way to success."

-*Ascribed to* Mickey Rooney [Yoseph Yule, Jun.], 1920-2014

"Failure changes for the better, success for the worst."

-Lucius Annaeus Seneca, c. 4 B.C.-65

"You may be disappointed if you fail, but you are doomed if you don't try."

-Beverly Sills [Belle Miriam Silverman], 1929-2007

"I cannot give you the formula for success, but I can give you the formula for failure, which is—try to please everybody."

-Herbert Bayard Swope, 1882-1958

"Being defeated is often a temporary condition. Giving up is what makes it permanent."

-Marlene vos Savant, 1946-

"Better an epic defeat than a tame victory."

-Anonymous

Faith

See also: Beliefs, Doubt, Religion

"To one who has faith, no explanation is necessary. To one without faith, no explanation is possible."

-*Ascribed to* Saint Thomas Aquinas, 1225-1274

"It wasn't raining when Noah built the ark."

-Howard J. Ruff, 1930-

"It is easy—terribly easy—to shake a man's faith in himself. To take advantage of that, to break a man's spirit is devil's work."

-George Bernard Shaw, 1856-1950

"The delicate in faith swiftly loose their assurance in the journey and join the false observation of happiness."

-*Ascribed to* John Zacary "Zac" Spencer, 1989-

"Faith which does not doubt is dead faith."

-Miguel de Unamuno, 1864-1936

"Martyrs create faith, faith does not create martyrs."

-Miguel de Unamuno, 1864-1936

"Now faith is the substance of things hoped for, the evidence of things not seen."

-The Epistle to the Hebrews 11:1

"He who has health has hope. And he who has hope has everything."

-Arabian proverb

Fame

See also: Admiration, Flattery, Glory, Praise, Respect

"Fame is proof that the people are gullible."

-Ascribed to Ralph Waldo Emerson, 1803-1882

"Fame is something like unto a kind of mushroom, which Pliny recounts to be the greatest miracle in nature, because growing and having no root, as fame no ground for her reports"

-Thomas Fuller, 1608-1661

"Fame sometimes hath created something of nothing."

-Thomas Fuller, 1608-1661

"Few great men could pass Personnel."

-Paul Goodman, 1911-1972

"Nothing arouses ambition so much...as the trumpet clang of another's fame."

-Baltasar Gracián, 1601-1658

"When smashing monuments, save the pedestals—they always come in handy."

-Stanislaw Jerzy Lec, Baron Z dnia Benon de Tusch-Letz, 1909-1966

"A celebrity is one who is known to many persons he is glad he doesn't know."

-Henry Louis Mencken, 1880-1956

"Fame is the thirst of youth."

-George Gordon Noel, 6th Baron Byron, 1788-1824

"Fame is the beginning of the fall of greatness."

-Ascribed to Vasily Vasilievich Rozanov, 1856-1919

"Love of fame is the last thing even learned men can bear to be parted from."

-Cornelius Tacitus, 56-120

"The final test of fame is to have a crazy person imagine he is you."

-Anonymous

Family

See also: Children, Humanity, Men, Parents, Relationships, Society, Women

"Cruel is the strife of brothers."

-Aristotle, 384-322 B.C.

"He that hath wife and children hath given hostages to fortune; for they are impediments to great enterprises, either of virtue or mischief."

-Sir Francis Bacon, 1561-1626

"He that has no fools, knaves, nor beggars in his family was begot by a flash of lightning."

-Dr. Thomas Fuller, 1654-1734

"Good families are generally worse than any others."

-Sir Anthony Hope [Anthony Hope Hawkins], 1863-1933

"The difference between us is that my family begins with me, whereas yours ends with you."

-Iphicrates, 419-348

"Few men have been admired by their own households."

-Michel Eyquem de Montaigne, 1533-1592

"After a certain age, the more one becomes oneself, the more obvious one's family traits become."

-Valentin Louis Georges Eugène Marcel Proust, 1871-1922

"A little more than kin, and less than kind."

-William Shakespeare, 1564-1616

"Happy families are all alike; every unhappy family is unhappy is its own way."

-Lev Nikolayevich "Leo" Tolstoy, Comte Tolstoy, 1828-1910

"Stupid sons don't ruin a family; it is the clever ones who do."

-Mr. Tut-Tut

"Do well and you will have no need of ancestors."

-*Ascribed to* Voltaire [François Marie Arouet], 1694-1778

Fear

See also Courage, Terrorism

"Severity breedeth fear, but roughness breedeth hate. Even reproofs from authority ought to be grave, and not taunting."

-Sir Francis Bacon

"The concessions of the weak are the concessions of fear."

-Edmund Burke, 1729-1797

"The heart which worries makes its owner ill."

-David Drake, 1945-

"Once men are caught up in an event they cease to be afraid. Only the unknown frightens men."

-Antoine de Saint Exupéry, 1900-1944

"Fear is the parent of cruelty."

-James Anthony Froude, 1818-1894

"Fear is maintained by dread of punishment, which never fails."

-Niccolò Machiavelli, 1469-1527

"I must be proud to see
Men not afraid of God, afraid of me."

-Alexander Pope, 1688-1744

"The only thing we have to fear is fear itself—nameless, unreasoning, unjustified terror which paralyzes needed efforts to convert retreat into advance."

-Franklin Delano Roosevelt, 1882-1945

"Present fears are less than horrible imaginings."

-William Shakespeare, 1564-1616

"We'll have a swashing and a martial outside, as many other mannish cowards have."

-William Shakespeare, 1564-1616

"To the man who is afraid everything rustles."

-Sophocles, 496-406 B.C.

"Conscience and cowardice are really the same things."

-Oscar Fingal O'Flahertie Wilde, 1854-1900

"The scalded dog fears hot water, and afterwards, cold."

-Italian proverb

"Fear leads you directly into the path of that which you fear."

-Anonymous

Flattery

See also: Admiration, Fame, Glory, Praise, Respect

"Charm is the quality in others that makes us more satisfied with ourselves."

-Henri Frédéric Amiel, 1821-1881

"If we would please in society, we must be prepared to be taught many things we know already by people who do not know them."

-Sebastien Roch Nicolas Chamfort, 1741-1794

"An endeavor to please elders is at the bottom of high marks and mediocre careers."

-John Jay Chapman, 1862-1933

"An appeaser is one who feeds a crocodile, hoping that it will eat him last."

-Sir Winston Leonard Spencer Churchill, 1874-1965

"Tact consists in knowing how far to go in going too far."

-Jean Maurice Eugène Clément Cocteau, 1889-1963

"Never trust a man who speaks well of everybody."

-*Ascribed to* John Churton Collins, 1848-1908

"All charming people have something to conceal, usually their total dependence on the appreciation of others."

-Cyril Vernon Connolly, 1903-1974

"Self-love is the greatest of all flatterers."

-François VI, Duc de La Rochefoucauld, 1613-1680

"Sometimes we think we dislike flattery, but it is only the way it is done that we dislike."

-François VI, Duc de La Rochefoucauld, 1613-1680

"A diplomatist is a man who always remembers a woman's birthday, but never remembers her age."

-*Ascribed to* Robert Lee Frost, 1874-1963

"Nothing is so silly as the expression of a man who is being complimented."

-André Paul Guillaume Gide, 1869-1951

"He who cannot love must learn to flatter."

-Johann Wolfgang von Goethe, 1749-1834

"Beware of the flatterer: He feeds you with an empty spoon."

-Cosino De Gregrio

"Tact is after all a kind of mind-reading."

-Sarah Orne Jewett, 1849-1909

"The flatterer does not think highly enough of himself or of others."

-Jean de La Bruyère, 1645-1695

"Be advised that all flatterers live at the expense of those who listen to them."

-Jean de La Fontaine, 1621-1695

"Tact is the art of convincing people that they know more than you do."

-Raymond Mortimer, 1895-1980

"He who knows how to flatter also knows how to slander."

-Napoléon I [Napoléon Bonaparte], 1769-1821

"Tact is the knack of making a point without making an enemy."

-Sir Isaac Newton, 1642-1727

"None are more taken in by flattery than the proud, who wish to be the first and are not."

-Benedict Spinoza, 1632-1677

"We recognize that flattery is poison, but its perfume intoxicates us."

-Charles Varlet, Marquis de La Grange, 1639-1692

"One can always be kind to people about whom one cares nothing."

-Oscar Fingal O'Flahertie Wilde, 1854-1900

"He that flatters you more than you desire either has deceived you or wishes to deceive."

-Italian proverb

"A flatterer is a man that tells you your opinion and not his own."

-Anonymous

"Social tact is making you company feel at home, even though you wish they were."

-Anonymous

Forgiveness

"It is a very delicate job to forgive a man, without lowering him in his estimation, and yours too."

-Josh Billings [Henry Wheeler Shaw], 1818-1885

"Once a woman has forgiven her man, she must reheat his sins for breakfast."

-Marlene Dietrich, 1904-1992

"There is a mercy which is weakness, and even treason against the common good."

-George Eliot [Marian Evans Cross], 1819-1880

"The weak can never forgive. Forgiveness is the attribute of the strong."

-Mohandas Karamchand Gandhi, 1869-1948

"The offender never pardons."

-George Herbert, 1593-1633

"If I have said something to hurt a man once, I shall not get the better of this by saying many things to please him."

-Dr. Samuel Johnson, 1709-1784

"He who excuses himself accuses himself."

-Gabriel Meurier, 1530-1601

"Mercy but murders, pardoning those that kill."

-William Shakespeare, 1564-1616

"Only the brave know how to forgive....A coward never forgave; it is not in his nature."

-Laurence Sterne, 1713-1768

"The stupid neither forgive nor forget; the naïve forgive and forget; the wise forgive but do not forget."

-Thomas Stephen Szasz, 1920-

"It is sometimes better to beg for forgiveness, rather than ask for permission."

-Anonymous

(Mis)Fortune

See also Adversity, Failure

"If a man looks sharply and attentively, he shall see fortune; for though she be blind, yet she is not invisible."

-Sir Francis Bacon, 1561-1626

"Calamities are of two kinds: misfortune to ourselves and good fortune to others."

-Ambrose Gwinnett Bierce, 1842-1914

"The common excuse of those who bring misfortune on others is that they desire good."

-Luc de Clapiers, Marquis de Vauvenargues, 1715-1747

"In the misfortune of our friends, we find something which is not displeasing to us."

-François VI, Duc de La Rochefoucauld, 1613-1680

"We all have strength enough to endure the misfortunes of others."

-François VI, Duc de La Rochefoucauld, 1613-1680

"We need greater virtues to sustain good fortune than bad."

-François VI, Duc de La Rochefoucauld, 1613-1680

"Fortune soon tires of carrying anyone long on her shoulders."

-Baltasar Gracián, 1601-1658

"The greatest reverses of fortune are the most easily borne from a sort of dignity belonging to them."

-William Hazlitt, 1778-1830

"The handwriting on the wall may be a forgery."

-Ralph Hodgson, 1871-1962

"Adversity has the effect of eliciting talents which, in prosperous circumstances, would have lain dormant."

-Horace [Quintus Horatius Flaccus], 65-8 B.C

"Acceptance of what has happened is the first step to overcoming the consequences of any misfortune."

-*Ascribed to* William James, 1842-1910

"All men's misfortunes spring form their hatred of being alone."

-Jean de La Bruyère, 1645-1695

"The shortest and best way to make your fortune is to let people see clearly that it is in their interests to promote yours."

-Jean de La Bruyère, 1645-1695

"It is better to be adventurous than cautious, because fortune is a woman."

-Niccolò Machiavelli, 1469-1527

"People don't ever seem to realize that doing what's right is no guarantee against misfortune."

-William McFee, 1881-1966

"Fortune does not change men; it unmasks them."

-*Ascribed to* Suzanne Curchod Necker, 1739-1794

"Fortune brings in some boats that are not steer'd."

-William Shakespeare, 1564-1616

"Fortune favors the brave."

-Virgil [Publius Vergilius Maro], 70-19 B.C.

"One likes people much better when they're battered down by a prodigious siege of misfortune than when they triumph."

-Virginia Woolf, 1882-1941

"Fortune favors the bold and abandons the timid."

-Latin proverb

Freedom

"So long as there is any subject which men may not freely discuss, they are timid upon all subjects."

-John Jay Chapman, 1862-1933

"Never claim as a right what you can ask as a favor."

-John Churton Collins, 1848-1908

"Liberty has not only enemies which it conquers, but perfidious friends, who rob the fruits of its victories: Absolute democracy, socialism."

-John Emerich Edward Dalberg, 1st Baron Acton, 1834-1902

"Liberty is not a means to a higher political end. It is itself the highest political end."

-John Emerich Edward Dalberg, 1st Baron Acton, 1834-1902

"The man who prefers his country before any other duty shows the same spirit as the man who surrenders every right to the State. They both deny that right is superior to authority."

-John Emerich Edward Dalberg, 1st Baron Acton, 1834-1902

"The most certain test by which we judge whether a country is really free is the amount of security enjoyed by minorities."

-John Emerich Edward Dalberg, 1st Baron Acton, 1834-1902

"Everything that emancipates the spirit without giving us control over ourselves is harmful."

-Johann Wolfgang von Goethe, 1749-1834

"Is life so dear, or peace so sweet, as to be purchased at the price of chains and slavery?"

-Patrick Henry, 1736-1799

"The last hope of human liberty in this world rests on us."

-Thomas Jefferson, 1743-1826

"The tree of liberty must be refreshed from time to time with the blood of patriots and tyrants. It is its natural manure."

-Thomas Jefferson, 1743-1826

"Censorship, like charity, should begin at home; but unlike charity, it should end there."

-Clare Booth Luce, 1903-1987

"None can love freedom heartily, but good men; the rest love not freedom, but license."

-John Milton, 1608-1674

"A man will fight harder for his interests than for his rights."

-Napoléon I [Napoléon Bonaparte], 1769-1821

"Liberty means responsibility. That is why most men dread it."

-George Bernard Shaw, 1856-1950

"When you have robbed a man of everything, he is no longer in your power. He is free again."

-Aleksandr Isayevich Solzhenitsyn, 1918-2008

Friends

See also Relationships

"Never take friendship personal."

-*Anberlin*, 2005

"A true friend is one who likes you despite your achievements."

-*Ascribed to* Enoch Arnold Bennett, 1867-1931

"We have three kinds of friends: those who love us, those who are indifferent to us, and those who hate us."

-Sebastien Roch Nicolas Chamfort, 1741-1794

"In prosperity our friends know us; in adversity we know our friends."

-John Churton Collins, 1848-1908

"Since we are mortal, friendships are best kept to a moderate level, rather than sharing the very depths of our souls."

-*Ascribed to* Euripides, 485-406 B.C.

"Friends will be your friends when it is convenient, but those who do so are not your friends."

-Brogan Lee Fullmer, 1988-

"Never have a companion who casts you in the shade."

-Baltasar Gracián, 1601-1658

"Love your neighbor; yet pull not down your hedge."

-George Herbert, 1593-1633

"The friendship that can cease has never been real."

-Saint Jerome, 342-420

"A true friend is one who overlooks your failures and tolerates your successes."

-Douglas L. Larson, 1926-

"Strange times lead to strange and fleeting friendships."

-Norman Ian Mackenzie, 1894-1986

"No guest is so welcome in a friend's house that he will not become a nuisance after three days."

-Titus Maccius Plautus, 254-184 B.C

"Every one's friend is no one's friend."

-Arthur Schopenhauer, 1788-1860

"Wiser, better, dearer than ourselves—such a friend ought to be."

-Mary Wollstonecraft Shelley, 1797-1851

"Treat your friend as if he might become an enemy."

-Publilius Syrus, first century B.C

"He makes no friend who never made a foe."

-Alfred Tennyson, 1st Baron Tennyson, 1809-1892

"A friend is one who knows all about you and likes you anyway."

-*Ascribed to* Christi Mary Warner

"A friend walks in when everyone walks out."

-Anonymous

"Good friends are like stars: you don't always see them, but you know they are always there."

-Anonymous

Future

See also Destiny

"You can never plan the future by the past."

-Edmund Burke, 1729-1797

"Everything in life is an omen."

-Paulo Coelho, 1947-

"The future belongs to God, and it is only he who reveals it, under extraordinary circumstances."

-Paulo Coelho, 1947-

"What we anticipate seldom occurs; what we least expected generally happens."

-Benjamin Disraeli, Earl of Beaconsfield, 1804-1881

"Cease to ask what the morrow will bring forth, and set down as gain each day that fortune grants."

-Horace [Quintus Horatius Flaccus], 65-8 B.C.

"The future is purchased by the present."

-Dr. Samuel Johnson, 1709-1784

"The best preparation [for the future] is the present well seen to, and the last duty done."

-George MacDonald, 1824-1905

"The future belongs to those who prepare for it."

-*Ascribed to* Malcolm X [Malcolm Little], 1925-1965

"The enemies of the future are always the very nicest people."

-Christopher Morley, 1890-1957

"The future doesn't belong to the fainthearted; it belongs to the brave."

-Ronald Wilson Reagan, 1911-2004

"The future belongs to those who believe in the beauty of their dreams."

-Anna Eleanor Roosevelt, 1884-1962

"The only limit to our realization of tomorrow will be our doubts of today. Let us move forward with strong and active faith."

-Franklin Delano Roosevelt, 1882-1945

"It is horrible to see everything that one detested in the past coming back wearing the colors of the future."

-Jean Rostand, 1894-1977

"Jesters do oft prove prophets."

-William Shakespeare, 1564-1616

"The future rests with the ones who tend the future."

-Sophocles, c. 496-406 B.C.

Genius

See also: Intelligence, Knowledge, Teaching, Wisdom

"Men of genius are rarely much annoyed by the company of vulgar people."

-Samuel Taylor Coleridge, 1772-1834

"Mediocrity can talk; but it is for genius to observe."

-Isaac D'Israeli, 1766-1848

"Colleges hate geniuses, just as convents hate saints."

-Ralph Waldo Emerson, 1803-1882

"Great geniuses have the shortest biographies: Their cousins can tell you nothing about them."

-Ralph Waldo Emerson, 1803-1882

"Genius, can be baffling. It isn't a product of intelligence or learning or discipline or training....it is instead an intuitive and spontaneous display of power that reasoning can never fathom."

-John Frederick Charles Fuller, 1878-1966

"Genius will live and thrive without training, but it does not the less reward the watering pot and pruning knife."

-Margaret Fuller [Sarah Margaret Fuller Ossoli], 1810-1850

"True genius walks along a line, and, perhaps, our greatest pleasure is in seeing it so often near falling, without being ever actually down."

-Oliver Goldsmith, 1728-1774

"Men of genius do not excel in any profession because they labor in it, but they labor in it because they excel."

-William Hazlitt, 1778-1830

"Genius is an infinite capacity for taking pains."

-Jane Ellis Hopkins, 1836-1904

"Genius...means little more than the faculty of perceiving in an inhabitable way."

-William James, 1842-1910

"What the world needs is more geniuses with humility, there are so few of us left."

-*Ascribed to* Oscar Levant, 1906-1972

"There is no great genius without some touch of madness."

-*Ascribed to* Lucius Annaeus Seneca, c. 4 B.C.-65

"When a true genius appears in the world, you may know him by this sign that the dunces are all in confederacy against him."

-Jonathan Swift, 1667-1745

"I've put my genius into my life; I've only put my talent into my works."

-Oscar Fingal O'Flahertie Wilde, 1854-1900

"There is a fine line between genius and insanity."

-Anonymous

Glory

See also: Admiration, Fame, Praise, Respect

"Thirst for glory is another phrase for ego worship."

-Pierre Corneille, 1606-1684

"The deed is everything, the glory nothing."

-Johann Wolfgang von Goethe, 1749-1834

"My dominant passion is certainly love of glory."

-Louis XIV [Louis-Dieudonné], 1638-1715

"Glory is fleeting, but obscurity is forever."

-Ascribed to Napoléon I [Napoléon Bonaparte], 1769-1821

"All glory comes from daring to begin."

-Anonymous

Goals

See also: Ambition, Desires, Dreams

"All that we do is done with an eye to something else."

-Aristotle, 384-322 B.C.

"You can't know where you're going till you know where you're at."

-Ascribed to Franz I [Franz Josef Carl Johann von Lothringen], 1768-1835

"A cathedral, a wave of a storm, a dancer's leap, never turn out to be as high as we had hoped."

-Valentin Louis Georges Eugène Marcel Proust, 1871-1922

"Fanaticism consists in redoubling your effort when you have forgotten your aim."

-George Santayana, 1863-1952

"In the long run, men hit only what they aim at."

-Henry David Thoreau, 1817-1862

74

"A man's capacity is usually relative to his goals."

> -From the Motion Picture *The Sea Chase*, 1955

"If you chase two rabbits, they will both escape."

> -Anonymous

God(s)

See also: Beliefs, Religion, Sin

"When obedience ceases to be an irritant and becomes our quest, in that moment God will endow us with power."

> -Ezra Taft Benson, 1899-1994

"The gods are those who either have money or do not want it."

> -Samuel Butler, 1835-1902

"Can one be a saint if God does not exist? That is the only concrete problem I know of today."

> -Albert Camus, 1913-1960

"Life is good, and God is in charge!"

> -Derek Alan Crimin, 1972-

"I do not feel obliged to believe that the same God who has endowed us with sense, reason, and intellect has intended us to forgo their use."

> -Galileo Galilei, 1564-1642

"Whoever obeys the gods, to him they particularly listen."

> -Homer, 700 B.C.

"Indeed, I tremble for my country when I reflect that God is just."

> -Thomas Jefferson, 1743-1826

"A man with God is always in the majority."

> -John Knox, c. 1513-1572

"If you have not chosen the kingdom of God, it will make in the end no difference what you have chosen instead."

-Clive Staples Lewis, 1898-1963

"Though the mills of God grind slowly; yet, they grind exceeding small."

-Friedrich von Logau, Freiherr von Logau, 1604-1655

"Do thy duty; that is best; Leave unto thy Lord the rest!"

-Henry Wadsworth Longfellow, 1807-1882

"The Spirit does not get our attention by shouting or shaking us with a heavy hand. Rather it whispers. It caresses so gently that if we are preoccupied we may not feel it at all."

-Boyd Kenneth Packer, 1924-

"The spiritual eyesight improves as the physical eyesight declines."

-*Ascribed to* Plato, c. 428-348 B.C.

"Those whom the gods love most grow young."

-Oscar Fingal O'Flahertie Wilde, 1854-1900

"When the gods wish to punish us they answer our prayers."

-Oscar Fingal O'Flahertie Wilde, 1854-1900

"A God all mercy is a God unjust."

-Edward Young, 1683-1765

"By night, an atheist half believes in God."

-Edward Young, 1683-1765

"Fear God, and keep his commandments: for this is the whole duty of man."

-*Ecclesiastes* 12:13

"Be not deceived; God is not mocked: For whatsoever a man soweth, that shall he also reap."

-*Epistle to the Galatians* 6:7

"God does not pay weekly, but he pays at the end."

-Dutch proverb

"In a small house God has His corner; in a big house, He has to stand in the hall."

-Swedish proverb

Good

See also: Evil, Morality, Sin, Vice, Virtue

"Those who act rightly are the ones who get the rewards and good things in life."

-Aristotle, 384-322 B.C.

"The wicked are always surprised to find that the good can be clever."

-Luc de Clapiers, Marquis de Vauvenargues, 1715-1747

"To go wrong in one's own way is better than to go right in someone else's."

-Fyodor Mikhailovich Dostoevsky, 1821-1881

"It's but little good you'll do a-watering the last year's crops."

-George Eliot [Marian Evans Cross], 1819-1880

"The time is always right to do what is right."

-Dr. Martin Luther King, Jun., 1929-1968

"It is not enough to do good; one must do it in a good way."

-John Morley, 1st Viscount Morley of Blackburn, 1838-1923

"Many people wait throughout their whole lives for the chance to be good in their own fashion."

-Friedrich Wilhelm Nietzsche, 1844-1900

"Keep true, never be ashamed of trying to do right; decide on what you think is right and stick to it."

-James Platt, 1831-?

"Men of ill judgment oft ignore the good that lies within their hands, till they have lost it."

-Sophocles, c. 496-406 B.C.

"There are two ways of spreading light: to be the candle or the mirror that reflects it."

-Edith Newbold Wharton, 1862-1937

"There's a strong streak of good in you, Superman. But then nobody's perfect, almost nobody."

-From the Motion Picture *Superman*, 1978

Government

See also: Leadership, Politics, Power

"The art of taxation consists in so plucking the goose as to get the most feathers with the least hissing."

-*Ascribed to* Jean Baptist Colbert, 1619-1683

"The point to remember is that what the government gives it must first take away."

-John Strider Coleman, 1897-1958

"The danger is not that one particular class is unfit to govern. Every class is unfit to govern."

-John Emerich Edward Dalberg, 1st Baron Acton, 1834-1902

"No government can be long secure without a formidable opposition."

-Benjamin Disraeli, Earl of Beaconsfield, 1804-1881

"Democracy becomes a government of bullies tempered by editors."

-Ralph Waldo Emerson, 1803-1882

"It is always much more difficult to arouse the attention of voters for a principle than for an interest."

-Dr. Erich Eyck, 1878-1964

"Peoples? What does that mean? I know only subjects."

-Franz I [Franz Josef Carl Johann von Lothringen], 1768-1835

"Rule and change nothing."

-Franz I [Franz Josef Carl Johann von Lothringen], 1768-1835

"Even though counting heads is not an ideal way to govern, it is better than breaking them."

-Billings Learned Hand, 1872-1961

"Take care that the Highest King does not strike you down because of the blindness that prevents you from governing justly."

-Saint Hildegard, 1098-1175

"There is no such thing as a little country. The greatness of a people is no more determined by their number than the greatness of a man is determined by his height."

-*Ascribed to* Victor Marie Hugo, 1802-1885

"Every great advance in natural knowledge has involved the absolute rejection of authority."

-Thomas Henry Huxley, 1825-1895

"Ask not what your country can do for you; ask what you can do for your country."

-John Fitzgerald Kennedy, 1917-1963

"Any acceptance of authority is the very denial of truth."

-Jiddu Krishnamurti, 1895-1986

"Anarchy is not chaos, but order with out control."

-*Ascribed to* David Layson

"If men were angels, no government would be necessary."

-James Madison, 1751-1836

"Unanimity is almost always an indication of servitude."

-*Ascribed to* Charles François Marie, Comte de Rémusat, 1797-1875

"He that would govern others first should be the master of himself."

-Phillip Massinger, 1583-1640

"Let the people think they govern, and they will be governed."

-William Penn, 1644-1718

"Democracy passes into despotism."

-Plato, c. 428-348 B.C.

"When there is an income tax, the just will pay more and the unjust less."

-Plato, c. 428-348 B.C.

"Government is not the solution to our problem; government is the problem."

-Ronald Wilson Reagan, 1911-2004

"As religion is imitated and mocked by hypocrisy, so public duty is parodied by patriotism."

-James Edwin Thorold Rogers, 1823-1890

"Democracy substitutes election by the incompetent many for appointment by the corrupt few."

-George Bernard Shaw, 1856-1950

Gratitude

See also Admiration, Respect

"Leave off wishing to deserve any thanks from anyone, thinking that anyone can ever become grateful."

-Galius Valerius Catullus, 87-54 B.C.

"Gratitude is a useless word. You will find it in a dictionary but not in life."

-*Ascribed to* François VI, Duc de La Rochefoucauld, 1613-1680

"It is no tragedy to do ungrateful people favors, but it is unbearable to be indebted to a scoundrel."

-*Ascribed to* François VI, Duc de La Rochefoucauld, 1613-1680

"The gratitude of most men is merely a secret desire to receive greater benefits."

-François VI, Duc de La Rochefoucauld, 1613-1680

"Too great haste in paying off an obligation is a kind of ingratitude."

-François VI, Duc de La Rochefoucauld, 1613-1680

"I now perceive one immense omission in my psychology—the deepest principle of Human Nature is the craving to be appreciated."

-William James, 1842-1910

"So much has been given to me. I have no time to ponder that which has been denied."

-Helen Adams Keller, 1880-1968

"Men in general are ungrateful and have less scruple in offending one who makes himself loved than one who makes himself feared."

-Niccolò Machiavelli, 1469-1527

"Gratitude is the most exquisite form of courtesy."

-Jacques Maritain, 1882-1973

"How sharper than a serpent's tooth it is to have a thankless child."

-William Shakespeare, 1564-1616

Habits

"All people are the same, only their habits differ."

-*Ascribed to* Confucius, 551-479 B.C.

"Cultivate only the habits that you are willing to master you."

-Elbert Green Hubbard, 1856-1915

"Habits form a second nature."

-*Ascribed to* Jean Baptise Lamarck, 1744-1829

"Be a good animal, true to your animal instincts."

-David Herbert Lawrence, 1885-1930

"One does what one is; one becomes what one does."

-Robert Musil, 1880-1942

"Ill habits gather by unseen degrees,
As brooks make rivers, rivers run to seas."

-Ovid, 43 B.C.-c. 17 A.D.

"To fall into habit is to begin to cease to be."

-Miguel de Unamuno, 1864-1936

"Why do we do what we do when we know what we know?"

-Anonymous

Happiness

See also Sadness

"The discovery of a new dish does more for human happiness than the discovery of a new star."

-Anthelme Brillat-Savarin, 1755-1826

"But what is happiness except the simple harmony between and man and the life he leads?"

-Albert Camus, 1913-1960

"To be happy, we must not be too concerned with others."

-Albert Camus, 1913-1960

"Those who have given themselves the most concern about the happiness of peoples have made their neighbors very miserable."

-Anatole France [Jacques Anatole François Thibault], 1844-1924

"Happiness makes up in height for what it lacks in length."

-Robert Lee Frost, 1874-1963

"Happy people are the only people, the rest are only human."

-Brogan Lee Fullmer, 1988-

"The soul that perpetually overflows with kindness and sympathy will always be cheerful."

-William Godwin, 1756-1836

"The true source of cheerfulness is benevolence."

-William Godwin, 1756-1836

"Many know how to please, but know not when they have to give pleasure."

-Sir Arthur Helps, 1813-1875

"We rarely find anyone who can say he has lived a happy life, and who, content with his life, can return from the world like a satisfied guest."

-Horace [Quintus Horatius Flaccus], 65-83 B.C.

"The supreme happiness in life is the conviction that we are loved."

-Victor Marie Hugo, 1802-1885

"Your success and happiness lie in you...Resolve to keep happy, and your joy and you shall form an invincible host against difficulties."

-Helen Adams Keller, 1880-1968

"Most men pursue pleasure with such breathless haste that they hurry past it."

-Søren Aabye Kierkegaard, 1813-1855

"We seek our happiness outside ourselves, and in the opinion of men we know to be flatterers, insincere, unjust, full of envy, caprice and prejudice."

-Jean de La Bruyère, 1645-1695

"A smile is the chosen vehicle for all ambiguities."

-Herman Melville, 1819-1891

"Amusement is the happiness of those that cannot think."

-Alexander Pope, 1688-1744

"It takes patience to appreciate domestic bliss; volatile spirits prefer unhappiness."

-George Santayana, 1863-1952

"The only way on earth to multiply happiness is to divide it."

-Paul Ehram Scherer, 1892-1969

"Happiness is nothing more than health and a poor memory."

-*Ascribed to* Dr. Albert Schweitzer, 1865-1965

"Oh, what a bitter thing it is to look into happiness through another man's eyes."

-William Shakespeare, 1564-1616

"We have no more right to consume happiness without producing it than to consume wealth without producing it."

-George Bernard Shaw, 1856-1950

"When falsehood can look so like truth, who can assure themselves of certain happiness?"

-Mary Wollstonecraft Shelley, 1797-1851

"Simple pleasures...are the last refuge of the complex."

-Oscar Fingal O'Flahertie Wilde, 1854-1900

"Happy endings are just stories that haven't finished yet."

-From the Motion Picture *Mr. & Mrs. Smith*, 2005

Hatred

See also: Admiration, Attitude, Jealousy, Praise, Respect

"If you hate a person, you hate something in him that is part of yourself. What isn't part of ourselves doesn't disturb us."

-Herman Hesse, 1877-1962

"Now hatred is by far the longest pleasure;
Men love in haste but they detest at leisure."

-George Gordon Noel, 6th Baron Byron, 1788-1824

"I will permit no man...to narrow and degrade my soul by making me hate him."

-Booker Taliaferro Washington, 1856-1915

Help

See also Charity

"To give real service you must add something which cannot be bought or measured with money and that thing is sincerity and integrity."

-Donald Allison Adams, 1881-?

"A fair request should be followed by the deed in silence."

-Dante Alighieri, 1265-1321

"The more help a person has in his garden, the less it belongs to him."

-William Henry Davies, 1871-1940

"What do we live for, if it is not to make life less difficult to each other?"

-George Eliot [Marian Evans Cross], 1819-1880

"You cannot do a kindness too soon, for you never know how soon it will be too late."

-Ralph Waldo Emerson, 1803-1882

"Most people return small favors, acknowledge medium ones, and repay great ones—with ingratitude."

-Dr. Benjamin Franklin, 1706-1790

"Remember that in giving any reason at all for refusing, you lay some foundation for a future request."

-Sir Arthur Helps, 1813-1875

"When a friend is in trouble, don't annoy him by asking if there is anything you can do; think up something appropriate, and do it."

-Edgar Watson Howe, 1853-1937

"The greatest pleasure I have known is to do a good action by stealth, and to have it found out by accident."

-Charles Lamb, 1775-1834

"Don't shout for help at night, you may wake your neighbors."

-Stanislaw Jerzy Lec, Baron Z dnia Benon de Tusch-Letz, 1909-1966

"Learn to say no. It will be of more use to you than to be able to read Latin."

-Charles Haddon Spurgeon, 1834-1892

"A favor well bestowed is almost as great an honor to him who confers it as to him who receives it."

-Sir Richard Steele, 1672-1729

"The sun doesn't give light to the moon assuming the moon's going to owe it one"

-*Linkin Park*, 2000

History

See also: Destiny, Future, Memories

"Think only of the past as its remembrance gives you pleasure."

-Jane Austen, 1775-1817

"A practical man is a man who practices the errors of his forefathers."

-Benjamin Disraeli, Earl of Beaconsfield, 1804-1881

"The century is advanced, but every individual begins afresh."

-Johann Wolfgang von Goethe, 1749-1834

"Perhaps in time the so-called Dark Ages will be thought of as including our own."

-*Ascribed to* Georg Christoph Lichtenberg, 1742-1799

"What is history but a fable agreed upon."

-*Ascribed to* Napoléon I [Napoléon Bonaparte], 1769-1821

"The best of prophets of the future is the past."

-George Gordon Noel, 6th Baron Byron, 1788-1824

"I tell you the past is a bucket full of ashes."

-Carl August Sandburg, 1878-1967

"Those who cannot remember the past are condemned to repeat it."

-George Santayana, 1863-1952

"What's past is prologue."

-William Shakespeare, 1564-1616

"Every beginning is a consequence—every beginning ends something."

-Ambroise-Paul-Toussaint-Jules Valéry, 1871-1945

"Everything that happens once can never happen again. But everything that happens twice will surely happen a third time."

-Arab proverb

"The reputation of a thousand years may be determined by the conduct of one hour."

-Japanese proverb

"History doesn't repeat itself, people repeat history."

-Anonymous

Honesty

See also: Deception, Lies, Truth, Trust

"He who says there is no such thing as an honest man, you may be sure is himself a knave."

-George Bishop Berkeley, 1685-1753

"'Tis my opinion every man cheats his way, and he is only honest who is not discovered."

-Susannah Centlivre, 1667-1723

"Weak people cannot be sincere."

-François VI, Duc de La Rochefoucauld, 1613-1680

"Integrity is praised and starves."

-Juvenal [Decimus Junius Juvenalis], 55-130 A.D.

"The surest way to remain poor is to be an honest man."

-Napoléon I [Napoléon Bonaparte], 1769-1821

"No legacy is so rich as honesty."

-William Shakespeare, 1564-1616

"To be honest, as this world goes, is to be one man picked out of ten thousand."

-William Shakespeare, 1564-1616

"Our culture peculiarly honors the act of blaming, which it takes as the sign of virtue and intellect."

-Lionel Trilling, 1905-1976

"To be sincere means to be the same person when one is with oneself; that is to say, alone—but that is all it means."

-*Ascribed to* Ambroise-Paul-Toussaint-Jules Valéry, 1871-1945

"There is no refuge from confession but suicide; and suicide is confession."

-Daniel Webster, 1782-1852

Humanity

See also Society

"Just when you think you have someone figured out, that's when they're most likely to surprise you."

-Haley Bogue, 1988-

"When the fight begins within himself, a man's worth something."

-Robert Browning, 1812-1889

"Man is the only animal that can remain on friendly terms with the victims he intends to eat until he eats them."

-Samuel Butler, 1835-1902

"Only remember that two-legged tigers and crocodiles are much more dangerous than those who walk on four."

-Alexandre Dumas, Père: [Dumas Davy de la Pailleterie], 1802-1870

"Nothing so much prevents our being natural as the desire to seem so."

-François VI, Duc de La Rochefoucauld, 1613-1680

"As I know more of mankind I expect less of them, and am ready now to call a man a good man upon easier terms than I was formerly."

-Dr. Samuel Johnson, 1709-1784

"No place affords a more striking conviction of the vanity of human hopes than a public library."

-Dr. Samuel Johnson, 1709-1784

"The educated man tries to repress the inferior one in himself, without realizing that by this he forces the latter to become revolutionary."

-Carl Gustav Jung, 1875-1961

"Human salvation lies in the hands of the creatively maladjusted."

-Dr. Martin Luther King, Jun., 1929-1968

"We must laugh at man, to avoid crying for him."

-Napoléon I [Napoléon Bonaparte], 1769-1821

"Man is equally incapable of seeing the nothingness from which he emerges and the infinity in which he is engulfed."

-Blaise Pascal, 1623-1662

"No human thing is of serious importance."

-Plato, c. 428-348 B.C.

"A man has generally the good or ill qualities which he attributes to mankind."

-William Shenstone, 1714-1763

"Many men are like unto sausages: Whatever you stuff them with, that they will bear in them."

-Alexi Konstantinovich Tolstoy, Comte Tolstoy 1817-1875

"He who can lick can bite."

-French proverb

Humor

See also Wit

"The marvelous thing about a joke with a double meaning is that it can only mean one thing."

-Ronald William George "Ronnie" Barker, 1929-2005

"No mind is thoroughly well organized that is deficient in a sense of humor."

-Samuel Taylor Coleridge, 1772-1834

"Serious things cannot be understood without laughable things, nor opposites at all without opposites."

-Plato, c. 428-348 B.C.

"Everything is funny as long as it is happening to somebody else."

-William Penn Adair "Will" Rogers, 1879-1935

"The joke loses everything when the joker laughs himself."

-Johann Christoph Friedrich von Schiller, 1775-1854

"You must not think me necessarily foolish because I am facetious, not will I consider you necessarily wise because you are grave."

-Sydney Smith, 1771-1845

"Nothing spoils a romance so much as a sense of humor in the woman."

-Oscar Fingal O'Flahertie Wilde, 1854-1900

Ideas

See also: Dreams, Opinions, Thoughts

"Nothing is more dangerous than an idea, when it's the only one we have."

-Émile-Auguste Chartier, 1868-1951

"Big ideas are so hard to recognize, so fragile, so easy to kill. Don't forget that, all of you who don't have them."

-*Ascribed to* John Elliot, Jun., 1937-

"Not only small men are changed by time and circumstances. The great men, too, who make history, are changed by their own ideas."

-Dr. Erich Eyck, 1878-1964

"Very simple ideas lie within the reach only of complex minds."

-Rémy de Gourmont, 1858-1915

"An invasion of armies can be resisted, but not an idea whose time has come."

-Victor Marie Hugo, 1802-1885

"If you are seeking creative ideas, go out walking. Angels whisper to a man when he goes for a walk."

-Raymond Inmon

"Ideas grow quickly, when watered with the blood of martyrs."

-Giuseppe Mazzini, 1805-1872

"Throughout history the world has been laid waste to ensure the triumph of conceptions that are now as dead as the men that died for them."

-Henry de Montherlant, 1896-1972

"We often refuse to accept an idea merely because the tone of voice in which it has been expressed is unsympathetic to us."

-*Ascribed to* Friedrich Wilhelm Nietzsche, 1844-1900

"A powerful idea communicates some of its power to the man who contradicts it."

-Valentin Louis Georges Eugène Marcel Proust, 1871-1922

"To each one of us, clear ideas are those which have the same degree of confusion as our own."

-Valentin Louis Georges Eugène Marcel Proust, 1871-1922

"Great ideas have a very short shelf life."

-John M. Shanahan, 1939-

"Having precise ideas often leads to a man doing nothing."

-*Ascribed to* Ambroise-Paul-Toussaint-Jules Valéry, 1871-1945

Image

"In great affairs men show themselves as they wish to be seen; in small things they show themselves as they are."

-Sebastien Roch Nicolas Chamfort, 1741-1794

"Appearances are not held to be a clue to the truth. But we seem to have no other."

-Dame Ivy Compton-Burnett, 1884-1969

"In order really to get to know any man, one must do it gradually and cautiously, so as not to fall into prejudice."

-Fyodor Mikhailovich Dostoevsky, 1821-1881

"Those who make their dress a principal part of themselves, will, in general, become of no more value than their dress."

-William Hazlitt, 1778-1830

"Eyes are more accurate witnesses than ears."

-Heraclitus, 540-480 B.C.

"What people say behind your back is your standing in the community."

-Edgar Watson Howe, 1853-1937

"He that hath the name to be an early riser may sleep till noon."

-James Howell, 1594-1666

"Early impressions are hard to eradicate from the mind. When once wool has been dyed purple, who can restore it to its previous whiteness?"

-Saint Jerome, 342-420

"It is necessary to be considered dangerous."

-Niccolò Machiavelli, 1469-1527

"One ought to be both feared and loved. But it is much safer to be feared than loved if one of the two has to be missing."

-Niccolò Machiavelli, 1469-1527

"It is easier to cope with a bad conscience than with a bad reputation."

-Friedrich Wilhelm Nietzsche, 1844-1900

"A fashion is nothing but an induced epidemic."

-George Bernard Shaw, 1856-1950

"Better keep yourself clean and bright; you are the window through which you see the world."

-George Bernard Shaw, 1856-1950

"An evil name—a drawback at first—sheds luster on old age."

-*Ascribed to* Logan Pearsall Smith, 1865-1946

"Our names are labels, plainly printed on the bottled essence of our past behavior."

-Logan Pearsall Smith, 1865-1946

"Either a good or a bad reputation outruns and gets before people wherever they go."

-Philip Dormer Stanhope, 4th Earl of Chesterfield, 1694-1773

"He that falls by himself never cries."

-Turkish proverb

"It is not what you wear; it is how you take it off."

-Anonymous

Imagination

See also Dreams, Thoughts

"Imagination is more important than knowledge."

-Albert Einstein, 1879-1955

"There is nothing more frightful than imagination without taste."

-Johann Wolfgang von Goethe, 1749-1834

"The key to life is imagination. If you don't have that, no matter what you have, it's meaningless."

-*Ascribed to* Jane Stanton Hitchcock, 1946-

"Were it not for imagination, sir, a man would be as happy in the arms of a chambermaid as of a duchess."

-Dr. Samuel Johnson, 1709-1784

"On the heights it is warmer than those in the valley imagine."

-Friedrich Wilhelm Nietzsche, 1844-1900

"Reality provides us with facts so romantic that imagination itself could add nothing to them."

-*Ascribed to* Jules Gabriel Verne, 1828-1905

"Discovery consists of seeing what everybody has seen and thinking what nobody has thought."

-Dr. Albert Szent-Györgyi, 1893-1936

"Consistency is the last refuge for the unimaginative."

-Oscar Fingal O'Flahertie Wilde, 1854-1900

Imitation

"Imitation is criticism."

-William Blake, 1757-1827

"We can say nothing but what hath been said. Our poets steal from Homer...Our story-dressers do as much; he that comes last is commonly best."

-Robert Burton, 1577-1640

"Trust yourself. Think for yourself. Act for yourself. Speak for yourself. Be yourself. Imitation is suicide."

-Marva Nettles Collins, 1936-

"Every man is a borrower and a mimic; life is theatrical and literature a quotation."

-Ralph Waldo Emerson, 1803-1882

"Whoso would be a man must be a nonconformist."

-Ralph Waldo Emerson, 1803-1882

"Always be a first-rate version of yourself and not a second-rate version of somebody else."

-Ascribed to Judy Garland [Frances Ethel Gumm], 1922-1969

"When people are free to do as they please, they usually imitate each other."

-Eric Hoffer, 1902-1983

"Almost all absurdity of conduct arises from the imitation of those whom we cannot resemble."

-Dr. Samuel Johnson, 1709-1784

"All the people like us are We, and everyone else is They."

-Joseph Rudyard Kipling, 1865-1936

"Individualism is rather like innocence: There must be something unconscious about it."

-Louis Kronenberger, 1904-1980

"To do just the opposite is also a form of imitation."

-Georg Christoph Lichtenberg, 1742-1799

"Whatever you may be sure of, be sure of this: That you are dreadfully like other people."

-James Russell Lowell, 1819-1891

"Men walk almost always in the paths of trodden by others, proceeding in their actions by imitation."

-Niccolò Machiavelli, 1469-1527

"Once conform, once do what others do because they do it, and a kind of lethargy steals over all the finer senses of the soul."

-Ascribed to Michel Eyquem de Montaigne, 1533-1592

"Man, as he is, is not a genuine article. He is an imitation of something, and a very bad imagination."

-Peter Demianovich Ouspensky, 1878-1947

"Every man becomes, to a certain degree, what the people he generally converses with are."

-Philip Dormer Stanhope, 4th Earl of Chesterfield, 1654-1773

"Originality is nothing but judicious imitation."

-Ascribed to Voltaire [François Marie Arouet], 1694-1778

"Most people are other people. Their thoughts are someone else's opinions, their lives a mimicry, their passions a quotation."

-Oscar Fingal O'Flahertie Wilde, 1854-1900

"If I try to be like him, who will be like me?"

-Yiddish proverb

"Only dead fish swim with the stream."

-Anonymous

"You can't roll around with the pigs without eventually smelling like them."

-Anonymous

Intelligence

See also: Education, Genius, Knowledge, Teaching, Wisdom

"A man is not necessarily intelligent because he has plenty of ideas, nay more than he is a good general because he has plenty of soldiers."

-Sebastien Roch Nicolas Chamfort, 1741-1794

"There is a kinship, a kind of freemasonry, between all persons of intelligence, however antagonistic their moral outlook."

-Norman Douglas, 1868-1952

"Our minds are lazier than our bodies."

-François VI, Duc de La Rochefoucauld, 1613-1680

"The intelligent man finds almost everything ridiculous, a wise man hardly anything."

-Johann Wolfgang von Goethe, 1749-1834

"I am somehow, less interested in the weight and convolutions of Einstein's brain, than in the near certainty that people of equal talent have lived and died in cotton fields and sweatshops."

-Stephen Jay Gould, 1941-2002

"Why should a man's mind have been thrown into such close, sad, sensational, inexplicable relations with such a precarious object as his body?"

-Thomas Hardy, 1840-1928

"The mind's direction is more important than its progress."

-Joseph Joubert, 1754-1824

"A collection of a hundred good intellects produces collectively one idiot."

-Carl Gutav Jung, 1875-1961

"Intellect is invisible to the man who has none."

-Arthur Schopenhauer, 1788-1860

"When a stupid man is doing something he is ashamed of, he always declares that it is his duty."

-George Bernard Shaw, 1856-1950

"Brains are an asset, if you hide them."

-Mary Jane "Mae" West, 1892-1980

"Artificial intelligence is no match for natural stupidity."

-Anonymous

Interests

"There are persons who, when they cease to shock us, cease to interest us."

-Francis Herbert Bradley, 1846-1924

"Your worst humiliation is only someone else's momentary entertainment."

-Karen Crockett

"Are you not scared by seeing that the gypsies are more attractive to us than the apostles?"

-Ralph Waldo Emerson, 1803-1882

"Tell me to what you pay attention and I will tell you who you are."

-*Ascribed to* José Ortega y Gasset, 1883-1955

"When a thing ceases to be a subject of controversy, it ceases to be a subject of interest."

-William Hazlitt, 1778-1830

"Little minds are interested in the extraordinary, great minds in the commonplace."

-Elbert Green Hubbard, 1856-1915

"You can't wait for inspiration. You have to go after it with a club."

-Jack London [John Griffith], 1896-1916

"No profit grows where is no pleasure taken; in brief, sir, study what you most affect."

-William Shakespeare, 1564-1616

Jealousy

See also: Admiration, Attitude, Hatred, Praise, Respect

"The jealous are the readiest of all to forgive, and all women know it."

-Fyodor Mikhailovich Dostoevsky, 1821-1881

"Jealousy, that dragon which slays love under the pretense of keeping it alive."

-Havelock Ellis, 1859-1939

"One of envy's favorite stratagems is the attempt to provoke envy in the envied one."

-Dr. Leslie H. Farber, 1912-1981

"In jealousy there is more self-love than love."

-François VI, Duc de La Rochefoucauld, 1613-1680

"Jealousy feeds upon suspicion, and turns into fury or it ends as soon as we pass form suspicion to certainty."

-François VI, Duc de La Rochefoucauld, 1613-1680

"Jealousy is always born with love, but does not always die with it."

-François VI, Duc de La Rochefoucauld, 1613-1680

"We often pride ourselves on even the most criminal passions, but envy is a timid and shamefaced passion we never dare to acknowledge."

-François VI, Duc de La Rochefoucauld, 1613-1680

"Nothing sharpens sight like envy."

-Dr. Thomas Fuller, 1654-1734

"Envy's a sharper spur than pay."

-John Gay, 1685-1732

"Envy honors the dead in order to insult the living."

-Claude-Adrien Helvétius, 1715-1771

"An envious heart makes a treacherous ear."

-Zora Neale Hurston, 1891-1960

"There is never jealousy where there is not strong regard."

-Washington Irving, 1783-1859

"Jealousy is the great exaggerator."

-Johann Christoph Friedrich von Schiller, 1775-1854

"Jealousy is the fear or apprehension of superiority; envy our uneasiness under it."

-William Shenstone, 1714-1763

"There is not a passion so strongly rooted in the human heart as envy."

-Richard Brinsley Sheridan, 1751-1816

"Man will do many things to get himself loved; he will do all things to get himself envied."

-Mark Twain [Samuel Langhorne Clemens], 1835-1910

"A show of envy is an insult to oneself."

-Yevgeny Alexandrovich Yevtushenko, 1933-

"Envy slays itself by its own arrows."

-Anonymous

Judgment

See also: Beliefs, Opinions, Thoughts

"It is well, when one is judging a friend, to remember that he is judging you with the same godlike and superior impartiality."

-Enoch Arnold Bennett, 1867-1931

"Who am I to judge, who am I to pass judgment on to other people?"

-Kobe Bean Bryant, 1978-

"By a small sample we may judge of the whole piece."

-Miguel de Cervantes [Miguel de Cervantes Saavedra], 1547-1616

"One has to observe a man for oneself, as closely as possible before one can judge him."

-Fyodor Mikhailovich Dostoevsky, 1821-1881

"It is the property of fools, to be always judging."

-Dr. Thomas Fuller, 1654-1734

"Knowledge is little; to know the right context is much; to know the right spot is everything."

-Hugo von Hofmannsthal, 1874-1929

"We judge ourselves by what we feel capable of doing, while others judge us by what we have already done."

-Henry Wadsworth Longfellow, 1807-1882

"There is no passion so much transports the sincerity of judgment as doth anger."

-Michel Eyquem de Montaigne-Michel Eyquem de Montaigne, 1533-1592

"Good judgment comes from experience, and experience comes from bad judgment."

-Gilbert Warren Nutter, 1923-1979

"My salad days, when I was green in judgment."

-William Shakespeare, 1564-1616

"The man who sees both sides of a question is a man who sees absolutely nothing at all."

-Oscar Fingal O'Flahertie Wilde, 1854-1900

"Never one to assume facts, not in evidence, you'll want to get more information, before you begin shaping your opinions and judgments."

-Anonymous

Justice

See also: Honesty, Judgment, Law

"I hear much of people's calling out to punish the guilty, but very few are concerned to clear the innocent."

-Daniel Defoe, 1660-1731

"The end justifies the means."

-Niccolò Machiavelli, 1469-1527

"A court is an assembly of noble and distinguished beggars."

-*Ascribed to* Charles Maurice, Comte de Talleyrand-Périgord, 1754-1838

"Injustice is relatively easy to bear; it is justice that hurts."

-Henry Louis Mencken, 1880-1956

"Fair is foul, and foul is fair."

-William Shakespeare, 1564-1616

"Time, and time alone will show the just man, though scoundrels are discovered in a day."

-Sophocles, c. 496-406 B.C.

"Every man is entitled to his hour in court."

-Japanese proverb

"'For example' is not proof."

-Yiddish proverb

Knowledge

See also: Education, Experience, Genius, Intelligence, Wisdom

"The fox knoweth many things, the hedgehog one great thing."

-Archilocus, c. 680-645 B.C.

"Mediocre men often have the most acquired knowledge."

-Claude Bernard, 1813-1878

"The things we know best are things we haven't been taught."

-Luc de Clapiers, Marquis de Vauvenargues, 1715-1747

"Seeking to know is only too often learning to doubt."

-Antoinette Du Ligier de la Garde Deshoulières, 1638-1694

"Mediocre minds usually dismiss anything which reaches beyond their own understanding."

-François VI, Duc de La Rochefoucauld, 1613-1680

"Only when we know little do we know anything; doubt grows with knowledge."

-Johann Wolfgang von Goethe, 1749-1834

"The world's great men have not commonly been great scholars, nor great scholars great men."

-Oliver Wendell Holmes, Sen., 1806-1894

"Most ignorance is invincible ignorance. We don't know because we don't want to know."

-Aldous Leonard Huxley, 1894-1963

"If a little knowledge is dangerous, where is the man who has so much as to be out of danger?"

-Thomas Henry Huxley, 1825-1895

"Knowledge is power...knowledge is safety...knowledge is happiness."

-Thomas Jefferson, 1743-1826

"The field of knowledge is the common property of all mankind."

-Thomas Jefferson, 1743-1826

"All that we know is nothing, we are merely crammed waste-paper baskets, unless we are in touch with that which laughs at all our knowing."

-David Herbert Lawrence, 1885-1930

"The most certain way to hide from others the limits of our knowledge is not to go beyond them."

-Giacomo Taldegardo Francesco Leopardi, Conte di Sales Saverio Pietro Leopardi, 1798-1837

"The greater the ignorance the greater the dogmatism."

-Sir William Osler, 1st Baronet Osler, 1849-1919

"We're drowning in information and starving for knowledge."

-Rutherford David Rogers, 1915-

"Of what a strange nature is knowledge! It clings to the mind, when it has once seized on it, like a lichen on the rock."

-Mary Wollstonecraft Shelley, 1797-1851

"Pocket all your knowledge with your watch and never pull it out in company unless desired."

-Philip Dormer Stanhope, 4th Earl of Chesterfield, 1694-1773

"The knowledge of the world is only to be acquired in the world, and not in a closet."

-Philip Dormer Stanhope, 4th Earl of Chesterfield, 1694-1773

"But desire of knowledge, like the thirst of riches, increases ever with the acquisition of it."

-Laurence Sterne, 1713-1768

"Go from the presence of a foolish man, when thou perceivest not in him the lips of knowledge."

-*The Proverbs* 14:7

"Ignorance is bliss."

-American proverb

Law

See also Judgment, Justice

"The law is reason free from passion."

-Aristotle, 384-322 B.C.

"Agree, for the law is costly."

-Sir William Camden, 1551-1623

"The law, in its majestic equality, forbids the rich as well as the poor to sleep under bridges, to beg in the streets, and to steal bread."

-Anatole France [Jacques Anatole François Thibault], 1844-1924

"Whatever their other contributions to our society, lawyers could be an important source of protein."

-*Ascribed to* Richard Gordon "Dick" Guindon, 1935-

"Rules and models destroy genius and art."

-William Hazlitt, 1778-1830

"The old law about an eye for an eye leaves everybody blind."

-Dr. Martin Luther King, Jun., 1929-1968

"There is no man so good that if he placed all the actions and thoughts under the scrutiny of the laws, he would not deserve hanging ten times in his life."

-Michel Eyquem de Montaigne, 1533-1592

"Laws are like cobwebs, which may catch small flies, but let wasps and hornets break through."

-Jonathan Swift, 1667-1745

"May you have a lawsuit in which you know you are in the right."

-Romani proverb

"It is better to be a mouse in a cat's mouth than a man in a lawyer's hands."

-Spanish proverb

"Law school is the opposite of sex. Even when it's good it's lousy."

-Anonymous

Leadership

See also: Government, Judgment, Trust

"My ambition strives more to command than to obey."

-Otto von Bismarck, 1st Herzog von Lauenburg, 1st Graf von Bismarck-Schönhausen, 1st Fürst von Bismarck 1815-1898

"Those who can, do; those who can't, teach; and those who can do neither, administer."

-*Ascribed to* Collet Calverley

"Wherever I sit is the head of the table."

-Miguel de Cervantes [Miguel de Cervantes Saavedra], 1547-1616

"Never assume that the herd must know where they are going, because they usually don't."

-Sean Covey, 1964-

"To get others to come into our ways of thinking, we must go over to theirs; and it is necessary to follow, in order to lead."

-William Hazlitt, 1778-1830

"I am more afraid of an army of one hundred sheep led by a lion that an army of one hundred lions led by a sheep."

-Charles Maurice, Comte de Talleyrand-Périgord, 1754-1838

"Never tell people how to do things. Tell them what to do and they will surprise you with their ingenuity."

-George Smith Patton, Jun., 1885-1945

"Consensus is the negation of leadership."

-Margaret Hilda Roberts Thatcher, 1st Baroness Thatcher, 1925-2013

"For those who govern, the first thing required is indifference to newspapers."

-Ascribed to Louis Adolphe Thiers, 1797-1877

"A leader cannot lead until he knows where he is going."

-Anonymous

Lies

See also: Deception, Honesty, Truth, Trust

"Some of the most frantic lies on the face of life are told with modesty and restraint; for the simple reason that only modesty and restraint will save them."

-Gilbert Keith Chesterton, 1874-1936

"All men are born truthful and die liars."

-Luc de Clapiers, Marquis de Vauvenargues, 1715-1747

"Remember: One lie does not cost you one truth but the truth."

-Ascribed to Christian Friedrich Hebbel, 1813-1863

"Show me a liar, and I'll show thee a thief."

-George Herbert, 1593-1633

"Men hate those to whom they have to lie."

-Victor Marie Hugo, 1802-1885

"There are times when lying is the most sacred of duties."

-Eugene Marin Labiche, 1815-1888

"He who does not need to lie is proud of not being a liar."

-Ascribed to Friedrich Wilhelm Nietzsche, 1844-1900

"One may sometimes tell a lie, but the grimace with which one accompanies it tells the truth."

-Ascribed to Friedrich Wilhelm Nietzsche, 1844-1900

"The visionary lies to himself, the liar only to others."

-Friedrich Wilhelm Nietzsche, 1844-1900

"If we suspect that a man is lying, we should pretend to believe him; for then he becomes bold and assured, lies more vigorously, and is unmasked."

-Arthur Schopenhauer, 1788-1860

"The cruelest lies are often told in silence."

-Robert Louis Balfour Stevenson, 1850-1894

"A lie is an abomination unto the Lord and a very present help is trouble."

-American proverb, *see reference*

"Who lies for you will lie against you."

-Bosnian proverb

"Clever liars give details, but the cleverest don't."

-Anonymous

Life

See also Death

"We need to find the courage to say NO to the things and people that are not saving us if we want to rediscover ourselves and live our lives with authenticity."

-*Ascribed to* Barbara De Angelis, 1951-

"To others we are not ourselves but a performer in their lives cast for a part we do not even know that we are playing."

-Elizabeth Bibesco, 1897-1945

"Life is so constructed, that the event does not, cannot, will not, match the expectation."

-Charlotte Brontë, 1816-1855

"Life is like playing a violin solo in public and learning the instrument as one goes along."

-Samuel Butler, 1835-1902

"Life is the art of drawing sufficient conclusions from insufficient premises."

-Samuel Butler, 1835-1902

"The tragedy of life is not so much what men suffer, but rather what they miss."

-*Ascribed to* Thomas Carlyle, 1795-1881

"Who well lives, long lives; for this age of ours should not be numbered by years, days, and hours."

-Guillaume de Salluste Du Bartas, 1544-1590

"There are moments which last a lifetime."

-Alexandre Dumas, Père [Dumas Davy de la Pailleterie], 1802-1870

"Life is a festival only to the wise."

-Ralph Waldo Emerson, 1803-1882

"The average man, who does not know what to do with his life, wants another one which will last forever."

-Anatole France [Jacques Anatole François Thibault], 1844-1924

"Be aware of wonder. Live a balanced life—learn some and think some and draw and paint and sing and dance and play and work every day some."

-Robert Lee Fulghum, 1937-

"The hell-fire of life consumes only the select among men. The rest stand in front of it, warming their hands."

-Christian Friedrich Hebbel, 1813-1863

"In nature, there are neither rewards nor punishments; there are consequences."

-Robert Greene Ingersoll, 1833-1899

"Life is not long, and too much of it must not pass in idle deliberation how it shall be spent."

-Dr. Samuel Johnson, 1709-1784

"The love of life is necessary to the vigorous prosecution of any undertaking."

-Dr. Samuel Johnson, 1709-1784

"In small proportions we just beauties see,
And in short measures life may perfect be."

-Ben Jonson, 1573-1637

"Life at court does not satisfy a man, but it keeps him from being satisfied with anything else."

-Jean de La Bruyère, 1645-1695

"Most men make use of the first part of their life to render the last part miserable."

-Jean de La Bruyère, 1645-1695

"We have multiplied our possessions, but reduced our values. We talk too much, love too seldom, and hate too often. We've learned how to make a living, but not a life."

-Dr. Robert Moorehead, 1937-?

"There are people who so arrange their lives that they feed themselves only on side dishes."

-José Ortega y Gasset, 1883-1955

"Repetition is the only form of permanence that nature can achieve."

-George Santayana, 1863-1952

"There is no cure for birth and death, save to enjoy the interval."

-George Santayana, 1863-1952

"Live to eat, don't eat to live."

-Tyson Robert Skeen, 1986-

"The unexamined life is not worth living."

-Socrates, 469-399 B.C.

"There is so much trouble in coming into the world, and so much more, as well as meanness, in going out of it, that 'tis hardly worth while to be here at all."

-Henry St John, 1st Viscount Bolingbroke, 1678-1751

"There is no more fatal blunder than he who consumes the greater part of his life getting his living."

-Henry David Thoreau, 1817-1862

"One's real life is often the life that one does not lead."

-Oscar Fingal O'Flahertie Wilde, 1854-1900

"Life is an unanswered question, but let's still believe in the dignity and importance of the question."

-Tennessee Williams [Thomas Lanier Williams III], 1911-1983

Literature

See also Writing

"In the case of good books, the point is not to see how many of them you can get through, but rather how many can get through to you."

-*Ascribed to* Mortimer Jerome Adler, 1902-2001

"The oldest books are still only just out to those who have not read them."

-Samuel Butler, 1835-1902

"At least half the mystery novels published violate the law that the solution, once revealed, must seem to be inevitable."

-Raymond Thornton Chandler, 1888-1959

"Some books seem to have been written, not to teach us anything, but to let us know that the author has known something."

-Johann Wolfgang von Goethe, 1749-1834

"Autobiography is an unrivaled vehicle for telling the truth about other people."

-Philip Guedalla, 1889-1944

"The proper place of an epic is in the storied past."

-Albert Léon Guérard, 1880-1959

"An autobiography is a preemptive strike against biographers."

-Barbara Grizzuti Harrison, 1934-2002

"Reading is sometimes an ingenious device for avoiding thought."

-Sir Arthur Helps, 1813-1875

"There be some men are born only to suck out the poison of books."

-Ben Jonson, 1573-1637

"A book is a mirror: If an ass peers into it, you can't expect an apostle to look out."

-Georg Christoph Lichtenberg, 1742-1799

"Reading means borrowing."

-Georg Christoph Lichtenberg, 1742-1799

"Literature is mostly about having sex and not much about having children; life is the other way round."

-David John Lodge, 1935-

"A work should contain its total meaning within itself and should impress it on the spectator before he even knows the subject."

-Henri Matisse, 1869-1954

"Deep vers'd in books and shallow in himself."

-John Milton, 1608-1674

"When we see a natural style we are quite amazed and delighted, because we expected to see an author and find a man."

-Blaise Pascal, 1623-1662

"If books could have more, be more...they would still need readers"

-Gary Paulson, 1939-

"A life being very short, and the quiet hours of it few, we ought to waste none of them in reading valueless books."

-John Ruskin, 1819-1900

"Weak men are the worse for the good sense they read in books because it furnisheth them only with more matter to mistake."

-George Savile, 1st Marquess of Halifax, 1633-1695

"Let blockheads read what blockheads wrote."

-Philip Dormer Stanhope, 4th Earl of Chesterfield, 1694-1773

"Books are good enough in their own way, but they are a mighty bloodless substitute for life."

-Robert Louis Balfour Stevenson, 1850-1894

"Biographies are but the clothes and buttons of the man—the biography of the man himself cannot be written."

-Mark Twain [Samuel Langhorne Clemens], 1835-1910

"'Classic': a book which people praise and don't read."

-Mark Twain [Samuel Langhorne Clemens], 1835-1910

"The man who does not read good books has no advantage over the man who can't read them."

-Mark Twain [Samuel Langhorne Clemens], 1835-1910

"The difference between journalism and literature is that journalism is unreadable and literature is not read."

-Oscar Fingal O'Flahertie Wilde, 1854-1900

"There is no such thing as a moral or an immoral book. Books are well written, or badly written."

-Oscar Fingal O'Flahertie Wilde, 1854-1900

"Books bear him up a while, and make him try to swim with bladders of philosophy."

-John Wilmot, 2nd Earl of Rochester, 1647-1680

"To me the charm of an encyclopedia is that it knows—and I needn't."

-Francis Yeats-Brown, 1886-1944

"A book is a success when people who haven't read it pretend they have."

-*Los Angeles Times*

Love

See also: Friendship, Hatred, Love, Men, and Women

"What is irritating about love is that it is a crime that requires an accomplice."

-Ascribed to Charles Baudelaire, 1821-1867

"Absence is to love what wind is to fire; it extinguishes the small, it inflames the great."

-Roger de Bussy-Rabutin, Comte de Bussy, 1618-1693

"Truly loving another means letting go of all expectations."

-Karen Casey, 1939-

"That's the nature of women...not to love when we love them, and to love when we love them not."

-Miguel de Cervantes [Miguel de Cervantes Saavedra], 1547-1616

"Love feeds upon leisure and grows by dint of corruption."

-Alexandre Dumas, Père [Dumas Davy de la Pailleterie], 1802-1870

"The human heart, at whatever age, opens only to the heart that opens in return."

-Maria Edgeworth, 1767-1849

"Of all the icy blasts that blow on love, a request for money is the most chilling and havoc-wreaking."

-Gustave Flaubert, 1821-1880

"In their first passion women love their lovers; in the other they love love."

-François VI, Duc de La Rochefoucauld, 1613-1680

"Lovers never get tired of each other, because they are always talking about themselves."

-François VI, Duc de La Rochefoucauld, 1613-1680

"There are very few people who are not ashamed of having been in love when they no longer love each other."

-François VI, Duc de La Rochefoucauld, 1613-1680

"There is no disguise which can for long conceal love where it exists or simulate it where it does not."

-François VI, Duc de La Rochefoucauld, 1613-1680

"True love is like ghosts, which everybody talks about and few have seen."

-François VI, Duc de La Rochefoucauld, 1613-1680

"Love, and a cough, cannot be hid."

-George Herbert, 1593-1633

"To act from pure benevolence is not possible for finite beings. Human benevolence is mingled with vanity, interest, or some other motive."

-Dr. Samuel Johnson, 1709-1784

"To cheat one's self out of love is the greatest deception of which there is no reparation in either time or eternity."

-Søren Aabye Kierkegaard, 1813-1855

"He who loves the more is the inferior and must suffer."

-Paul Thomas Mann, 1875-1955

"Love is a dirty trick played on us to achieve the continuation of the species."

-William Somerset Maugham, 1874-1965

"Man's love is of man's life a thing apart; 'tis woman's whole existence."

-George Gordon Noel, 6th Baron Byron, 1788-1824

"To be able to say how much you love is to love but little."

-Petrarch [Francesco Petrarca], 1304-1374

"It is a mistake to speak of a bad choice in love, since, as soon as the choice exists, it can only be bad."

-Valentin Louis Georges Eugène Marcel Proust, 1871-1922

"There can be no peace of mind in love, since the advantage one has secured is never anything but a fresh starting-point for further desires."

-Valentin Louis Georges Eugène Marcel Proust, 1871-1922

"Loving goes by haps:
Some Cupid kills with arrows, some with traps."

-William Shakespeare, 1564-1616

"Love is the whole history of a woman's life; it is but an episode in a man's."

-Madame de Staël, Barrone de Staël-Holstein [Anne Louise Germaine de Staël-
Holstein], 1766-1817

"'Tis better to have loved and lost
Than never to have loved at all."

-Alfred Tennyson, 1st Baron Tennyson 1809-1892

"It would be impossible to 'love' anyone or anything one knew completely. Love is
directed towards what lies hidden in its object."

-Ambroise-Paul-Toussaint-Jules Valéry, 1871-1945

"There is a land of the living and a land of the dead, and the bridge is love."

-Thornton Niven Wilder, 1897-1975

"Love lodged in a woman's breast is but a guest."

-Sir Henry Wotton, 1568-1639

"There is one who kisses, and the other who offers the cheek."

-French proverb

Luck

See also Chance, (Mis)Fortune

"Luck is being ready for the chance."

-*Ascribed to* James Frank Dobie, 1888-1964

"Those who mistake their good luck for their merit are inevitably bound for disaster."

-Jean Christopher Herold, 1919-1964

"Some people are so fond of ill luck that they run halfway to meet it."

-Douglas William Jerrold, 1803-1857

"Luck is a matter of preparation meeting opportunity."

-Elmer G. Leterman, 1897-1982

"Luck affects everything. Let your hook always be cast; in the stream where you least expect it, there will be a fish."

-Ovid [Publius Ovidius Naso], 43 B.C-18 A.D.

"There was a star that danced, and under that was I born."

-William Shakespeare, 1564-1616

"Luck is infatuated with the efficient."

-Persian proverb

"Luck never gives; it only lends."

-Swedish proverb

Manners(isms)

See also Habits

"Artificial manners vanish the moment the natural passions are touched."

-Maria Edgeworth, 1767-1849

"The test of good manners is to be patient with bad ones."

-*Ascribed to* Solomon ben Yehuda ibn Gabirol, 1022-1070

"A man's manners are a mirror in which he shows his portrait."

-Johann Wolfgang von Goethe, 1749-1834

"The reasons which any man offers to you for his own conduct betray his opinion of your character."

-Sir Arthur Helps, 1813-1875

"Those whose conduct gives room for talk are always the first to attack their neighbors."

-Molière [Jean-Baptiste Poquelin], 1622-1673

"Manners are a sensitive awareness of the feelings of others. If you have that awareness, you have good manners, no matter what fork you use."

-Ascribed to Emily Post, 1873-1960

"The gentle mind by gentle deeds is known. For a man by nothing is so well betrayed, as by his manners."

-Edmund Spenser, 1552-1599

Marriage

See also: Love, Men, Women

"Marriage, *noun*. The state or condition of a community consisting of a master, a mistress, and two slaves, making in all, two."

-Ambrose Gwinnett Bierce, 1842-1914

"Marriage is the only war in which you sleep with the enemy."

-Ascribed to François VI, Duc de La Rochefoucauld, 1613-1680

"Keep your eyes wide open before marriage, half shut afterwards."

-Dr. Benjamin Franklin, 1706-1790

"A happy home is one in which each spouse grants the possibility that the other may be right, though neither believes it."

-Don MacKay Fraser, 1946-1985

"To marry a second time represents the triumph of hope over experience."

-Dr. Samuel Johnson, 1709-1784

"In olden times sacrifices were made at the alter, a custom which is still continued."

-Helen Rowland, 1875-1950

"If thou wilt needs marry, marry a fool; for wise men know well enough what monsters you make of them."

-William Shakespeare, 1564-1616

"There are three important steps in a man's life: birth, marriage, and death...but not necessarily in that order."

-John M. Shanahan, 1939-

"When two people are under the influence of the most violent, most insane, most delusive, and most transient of passions, they are required to swear that they will remain in that excited, abnormal, and exhausting condition continuously until death do them part."

-George Bernard Shaw, 1856-1950

"It takes a loose rein to keep a marriage tight."

-*Ascribed to* John Stevenson

"The one charm of marriage is that it makes a life of deception absolutely necessary for both parties."

-Oscar Fingal O'Flahertie Wilde, 1854-1900

"Who follows his wife in everything is an ignoramus."

-The *Talmud*

"It is slavery and a disgrace if a wife supports her husband."

-Anonymous

Memories

See also History

"Memory, however tortuous, is less oppressive than a living creature."

-Alexandre Dumas, Père [Dumas Davy de la Pailleterie], 1802-1870

"Women forget all those things they don't want to remember."

-Zora Neale Hurston, 1891-1960

"To endeavor to forget anyone is a certain way of thinking of nothing else."

-Jean de La Bruyère, 1645-1695

"Some people do not become thinkers simply because their memories are too good."

-*Ascribed to* Friedrich Wilhelm Nietzsche, 1844-1900

"We are linked by blood, and blood is memory without language."

-Joyce Carol Oates, 1938-

"A very great memory often forgetteth how much time is lost by repeating things of no use."

-George Savile, 1st Marquess of Halifax, 1633-1695

"Could we know what men are most apt to remember, we might know what they are most apt to do."

-George Savile, 1st Marquess of Halifax, 1633-1695

"When I was younger I could remember anything whether it happened or not."

-Mark Twain [Samuel Langhorne Clemens], 1835-1910

"What was hard to endure is sweet to recall."

-Continental proverb

"To want to forget something is to think of it."

-French proverb

Men

See also: Humanity, Relationships, Society, Women

"You never know till you try to reach them how accessible men are; but you must approach each man by the right door."

-Henry Ward Beecher, 1813-1887

"Anybody who believes that the way to a man's heart is through his stomach flunked geography."

-Robert Byrne, 1930-

"Men are what their mothers made them."

-Ralph Waldo Emerson, 1803-1882

"Men, in general, are but great children."

-*Ascribed to* Napoléon I [Napoléon Bonaparte], 1769-1821

"There are two levers for moving men: interest and fear."

-*Ascribed to* Napoléon I [Napoléon Bonaparte], 1769-1821

Mistakes

See also Effort, Success

"No one is more liable to make mistakes than the man who acts only on reflection."

-Luc de Clapiers, Marquis de Vauvenargues, 1715-1747

"Who lives without folly is not so wise as he thinks."

-François VI, Duc de La Rochefoucauld, 1613-1680

"The small demerit extinguishes a long service."

-Dr. Thomas Fuller, 1654-1734

"We are not satisfied to be right, unless we can prove others to be quite wrong."

-William Hazlitt, 1778-1830

"The greatest mistake you can make in life is to be continually fearing you will make one."

-Elbert Green Hubbard, 1856-1915

"Great blunders are often made, like large ropes, of a multitude of fibers."

-Victor Marie Hugo, 1802-1885

"The ultimate result of shielding men form the effects of folly is to fill the world with fools."

-Herbert Spencer, 1820-1903

"If you shut your door to all errors, truth will be shut out."

-Rabindranath Tagore, 1861-1941

"Error is a hardy plant: If flourisheth in every soil."

-Martin Farquhar Tupper, 1810-1889

Morality

See also: Deception, Lies, Sin, Truth, Trust

"Moral virtue comes about as a result of practice."

-Aristotle, 384-322 B.C.

"Moral indignation is in most cases two percent moral, forty-eight percent indignation, and fifty percent envy."

-Vittorio De Sica, 1901-1974

"No one knows what he is doing so long as he is acting rightly; but of what is wrong one is always conscious."

-Johann Wolfgang von Goethe, 1749-1834

"Whatever you condemn, you have done yourself."

-Georg Groddeck, 1866-1934

"Most people have seen worse things in private than they pretend to be shocked at in public."

-Edgar Watson Howe, 1853-1937

"Prudery is half a virtue and half a vice."

-Victor Marie Hugo, 1802-1885

"The arm of the moral universe is long, but it bends toward injustice."

-Dr. Martin Luther King, Jun., 1929-1968

"The people who are regarded as moral luminaries are those who forego ordinary pleasures themselves and find compensation in interfering with the pleasures of others."

-Bertrand Arthur William Russell, 3rd Earl of Russell, 1872-1970

"There is nothing either good or bad, but thinking makes it so."

-William Shakespeare, 1564-1616

"Ethical man: A Christian holding four aces."

-Ascribed to Mark Twain [Samuel Langhorne Clemens], 1835-1910

"Women are the wild life of a country: Morality corresponds to game laws."

-Anonymous

Music

See also Art

"Classical music is the kind we keep thinking will turn into a tune."

-Frank McKinney "Kin" Hubbard, 1868-1930

"Learning music by reading about it is like making love by mail."

-Luciano Pavarotti, 1935-2007

"Hell is full of musical amateurs: music is the brandy of the damned."

-George Bernard Shaw, 1856-1950

"It is easier to understand a nation by listening to its music than by learning its language."

-Anonymous

Opinions

See also Ideas, Thoughts

"I often marvel how it is that though each man loves himself beyond all else, he should yet value his own opinion of himself less than that of others."

-Marcus Aurelius, 121-180

"Opinions have vested interests just as men have."

-Samuel Butler, 1835-1902

"Our enemies approach nearer to truth in their judgments of us than we do ourselves."

-François VI, Duc de La Rochefoucauld, 1613-1680

"All the world is competent to judge my pictures except those who are of my profession."

-*Ascribed to* William Hogarth, 1697-1764

"Those who never retract their opinions love themselves more than they love the truth."

-Joseph Joubert, 1754-1824

"There are two sides to every question: my side and the wrong side."

-*Ascribed to* Oscar Levant, 1906-1972

"It is a golden rule not to judge men by their opinions but rather by what their opinions make of them."

-Georg Christoph Lichtenberg, 1742-1799

"Opinions cannot survive if one has no chance to fight for them."

-Paul Thomas Mann, 1875-1955

"We probably wouldn't worry about what people think of us if we could know how seldom they do."

-Olin Miller

"The world is ruled by force, not by opinion; but opinion uses force."

-Blaise Pascal, 1623-1662

"Men who borrow their opinions can never repay their debts."

-George Savile, 1st Marquess of Halifax, 1633-1695

"What others think of us would be of little moment did it not, when known, so deeply tinge what we think of ourselves."

-Lucius Annaeus Seneca, c. 4 B.C.-65

"It is as proper to our age to cast beyond ourselves in our opinions as it is common for the younger sort to lack discretion."

-William Shakespeare, 1564-1616

"Opinion is ultimately determined by the feelings, and not by the intellect."

-Herbert Spencer, 1820-1903

"Conscience is, in most men, an anticipation of the opinion of others."

-Sir Henry Taylor, 1800-1886

"It were not best that we should all think alike; it is difference of opinion that makes horse-races."

-Mark Twain [Samuel Langhorne Clemens], 1835-1910

"One often makes a remark and only later sees how true it is."

-*Ascribed to* Ludwig Josef Johann Wittgenstein, 1889-1951

"The man who can't dance thinks the band is no good."

-Polish proverb

Opportunity

See also Chance

"The best you get is an even break."

-Franklin Pierce Adams, 1868-1941

"A wise man will make more opportunities than he finds."

-Sir Francis Bacon, 1561-1626

"When one door close, another opens; but we often look so long and so regretfully upon the closed door that we do not see the one which has opened for us."

-*Ascribed to* Alexander Graham Bell, 1847-1922

"Opportunity is sometimes hard to recognize if you're only looking for a lucky break."

-Monta Mildred? Crane, 1911?-2009?

"Next to knowing when to seize an opportunity, the most important thing in life is to know when to forgo an advantage."

-Benjamin Disraeli, Earl of Beaconsfield, 1804-1881

"Time is the father of opportunity; opportunity is the martingale of man."

-Alexandre Dumas, Père [Dumas Davy de la Pailleterie], 1802-1870

"No great man ever complains of want of opportunity."

-Ralph Waldo Emerson, 1803-1882

"History shows that neglected opportunities, as a rule, do not return."

-Dr. Erich Eyck, 1878-1964

"The mill cannot grind with the water that's past."

-George Herbert, 1593-1633

"Opportunities are usually disguised as hard work, so most people don't recognize them."

-Ann Landers [Esther Pauline Friedman Lederer], 1918-2002

"One can present people with opportunities. One cannot make them equal to them."

-Rosamond Lehmann, 1901-1990

"Equality of opportunity means equal opportunity to be unequal."

-Fiona MacLeod [William Sharp], 1855-1905

"It is not impossibilities which fill us with the deepest despair, but possibilities which we have failed to realize."

-*Ascribed to* Robert Mallet, 1915-2002

"Unless a man has trained himself for his chance, the chance will only make him ridiculous."

-*Ascribed to* William Matthews, 1942-1997

"Wherever we look upon this earth, the opportunities take shape within the problems."

-Nelson Rockefeller, 1908-1979

"Doors don't slam open."

-John M. Shanahan, 1939-

"Opportunity does not come to pass if we want it to; it is continuous, we take it as we become aware of it."

-*Ascribed to* John Zacary "Zac" Spencer, 1989-

"While we stop to think, we often miss our opportunity."

-Publilius Syrus, first century B.C.

"Opportunity's favorite disguise is trouble."

-Frank Tyger, 1929-2011

"Everyone is born a king, and most people die in exile."

-Oscar Fingal O'Flahertie Wilde, 1854-1900

"There are many things that we would throw away, if we were not afraid that others might pick them up."

-Oscar Fingal O'Flahertie Wilde, 1854-1900

"Enjoy your ice cream while it's on your plate."

-Thornton Niven Wilder, 1897-1975

"If your ship doesn't come in, swim out to it!"

-Jonathan Harshman Winters III, 1925-2013

Parents

See also: Children, Humanity, Men, Relationships, Society, Women

"The joys of parents are secret, and so are their grief's and fears."

-Sir Francis Bacon, 1561-1626

"A hen is only an egg's way of making another egg."

-Samuel Butler, 1835-1902

"You don't have to deserve your mother's love. You have to deserve your father's. He's more particular."

-Robert Lee Frost, 1874-1963

"Rarely are sons similar to their fathers; most are worse, and a few are better than their fathers."

-Homer, 700 B.C.

"Greatness of name, in the father, oft times helps not forth, but overwhelms the son: They stand too near one another. The shadow kills the growth."

-Ben Jonson, 1573-1637

"Nothing is a stronger influence psychologically on their environment, and especially on their children, than the unveiled lives of the parents."

-Carl Gustav Jung, 1875-1961

"All women become like their mothers. That is their tragedy. No man does. That's his."

-Oscar Fingal O'Flahertie Wilde, 1854-1900

"Children begin by loving their parents; as they grow older they judge them; sometimes they forgive them."

-Oscar Fingal O'Flahertie Wilde, 1854-1900

"A father is a banker provided by nature."

-Anonymous

"The affection of a father and a son are different: The father loves the person of the son, and the son loves the memory of his father."

-Anonymous

Passions

See also: Habits, Happiness, Interests, Love

"All passions exaggerate: It is only because they exaggerate that they are passions."

-Sebastien Roch Nicolas Chamfort, 1741-1794

"Popular passion never likes cold logic."

-Dr. Erich Eyck, 1878-1964

"Absence diminishes mediocre passions and increases great ones, as the wind blows out candles and fans fire."

-François VI, Duc de La Rochefoucauld, 1613-1680

"In the human heart new passions are forever being born; the overthrow of one almost always means the rise of another."

-François VI, Duc de La Rochefoucauld, 1613-1680

"We may affirm absolutely that nothing great in the world has been accomplished without passion."

-Georg Wilhelm Friedrich Hegel, 1770-1831

"It is with our passions as it is with fire and water; they are good servants but bad masters."

      -Sir Roger L'Estrange, 1616-1704

"It is difficult to overcome one's passions, and impossible to satisfy them."

      -Marguerite Hessein de La Sablière, c. 1640-1693

"An emotion ceases to be a passion as soon as we form a clear and distinct idea of it."

      -Benedict Spinoza, 1632-1677

"When you have found out the prevailing passion of any man, remember never to trust him where that passion is concerned."

      -Philip Dormer Stanhope, 4th Earl of Chesterfield, 1694-1773

"To know your ruling passion, examine your castles in the air."

      -Richard Whately, Archbishop of Dublin, 1787-1863

"The only difference between a caprice and a lifelong passion is that the caprice lasts a little longer."

      -Oscar Fingal O'Flahertie Wilde, 1854-1900

Patience

"Tolerance is the eager and glad acceptance of the way along which others seek the truth."

      -*Ascribed to* Sir Walter Besant, 1836-1901

"Beware the fury of a patient man."

      -John Dryden, 1631-1700

"Patience has its limits. Take it too far, and it's cowardice."

      -George Jackson, 1941-1971

"All the trouble in the world is due to the fact that men cannot sit still in a room."

      -Blaise Pascal, 1623-1662

"In any contest between power and patience, bet on patience."

      -*Ascribed to* W.B. Prescott

"He that knows patience knows peace."

-Chinese proverb

"People count up the faults of those who are keeping them waiting."

-French proverb

"Waiting is mindless. It suggests that there is no way to enjoy what is being done at the moment."

-Anonymous

Patriotism

See also Government, Politics

"And say not thou, 'My country right or wrong,' Nor shed blood for an unhallowed cause."

-*Ascribed to* John Quincy Adams, 1767-1848

"Patriotism is a lively sense of collective responsibility. Nationalism is a silly cock crowing on its own dunghill."

-Edward Godfree "Richard" Aldington, 1892-1962

"A wise man's country is the world."

-Aristippus, 435-356 B.C.

"What is subversive to-day will almost certainly be patriotic to-morrow."

-Lucius Morris Beebe, 1902-1966

"Loyalty must arise spontaneously from the hearts of people who love their country and respect their government."

-Hugo LaFayette Black, 1886-1971

"Surely the hero whose name is splashed in headlines for some singular spectacular deed of valor is no more a patriot than the unknown, steadfast citizen who year after year quietly and unselfishly benefits his nation."

-*Ascribed to* Albert Carr

"Patriots are grown too shrewd to be sincere, and we too wise to trust them."

-William Cowper, 1731-1800

"Patriotism is when love of your own people comes first; nationalism, when hate for people other than your own comes first."

-Charles André Joseph Marie de Gaulle, 1890-1970

"True patriotism does not exclude an understanding of the patriotism of others."

-Elizabeth II [Elizabeth Alexandra Mary Windsor], 1926-

"Love for one's country which is not a part of one's love for humanity is not love, but idolatrous worship."

-Erich Pinchas Fromm, 1900-1980

"One of the great attractions of patriotism—it fulfills our worst wishes. In the person of our nation we are able, vicariously, to bully and cheat, what's more, with a feeling that we are profoundly virtuous."

-Aldous Leonard Huxley, 1894-1963

"Patriotism is the willingness to kill and be killed for trivial reasons."

-Bertrand Arthur William Russell, 3rd Earl of Russell, 1872-1970

"Our country, right or wrong. When right to be kept right; when wrong to be put right."

-Carl Schurtz, 1829-1906

"No other factor in history, not even religion, has produced so many wars as has the clash of national egotism sanctified by the name of patriotism."

-Dr. Preserved Smith, 1880-1941

"There is no glory like his who saves his country."

-Alfred Tennyson, 1st Baron Tennyson 1809-1892

"In the beginning of a charge, the patriot is a scarce man, and brave, and hated, and scorned. When his cause succeeds, the timid join him, for then it costs nothing to be a patriot."

-Mark Twain [Samuel Langhorne Clemens], 1835-1910

"A real patriot is the fellow who gets a parking ticket and rejoices that the system works."

-*Ascribed to* William E. "Bill" Vaughan, 1915-1977

"Everybody likes to hear about a man laying down his life for his country, but nobody wants to hear about a country giving her shirt for her planet."

-Elwyn Brooks White, 1899-1985

"Patriotism is the virtue of the vicious."

-Oscar Fingal O'Flahertie Wilde, 1854-1900

"An honest patriot today may feel extremely virtuous, but he is none the less an anachronism wandering about a powder-magazine with a torchlight."

-*Ascribed to* Ida Alexa Ross Wylie, 1885-1959

Peace

See also: Conflict, Enemies, War

"I think that people want peace so much that one of these days government had better get out of their way and let them have it."

-Dwight David "Ike" Eisenhower, 1890-1969

"He is happiest, be he king or peasant who finds peace in his home."

-Johann Wolfgang von Goethe, 1749-1834

"Genuine harmony must come from the heart. It cannot come from the barrel of a gun."

-Tenzin Gyatso, 14th Dalai Lama, 1935-

"Nobody forgets where he buried the hatchet."

-Frank McKinney "Kin" Hubbard, 1868-1930

"Be on your guard against a silent dog and still water."

-Latin proverb

(Im)Perfection

See also: Achievement, Adversity, Talent

"Only mediocrity can be trusted to be always at its best."

-Sir Henry Maximilian Beerbohm, 1872-1956

"It is the nature of all greatness not to be exact."

-Edmund Burke, 1729-1797

"I cling to my imperfection, as the very essence of my being."

-Anatole France [Jacques Anatole François Thibault], 1844-1924

"The greatest grossness sometimes accompanies the greatest refinement, as a natural relief."

-William Hazlitt, 1778-1830

"I don't want to see the uncut version of anything."

-Bridget Jean Kerr, 1922-2003

"One of the misfortunes of our time is that in getting rid of false shame, we have killed off so much real shame as well."

-Louis Kronenberger, 1904-1980

"Perfect behavior is born of complete indifference."

-Cesare Pavese, 1908-1950

"Striving to better, oft we mar what's well."

-William Shakespeare, 1564-1616

"'The best' is an impossibility that only God can overcome."

-*Ascribed to* John Zacary "Zac" Spencer, 1989-

"God made everything out of nothing. But the nothingness shows through."

-Ambroise-Paul-Toussaint-Jules Valéry, 1871-1945

Philosophy

See also: Beliefs, Reasoning, Thought

"It distresses me, this failure to keep pace with the leaders of thought, as they pass into oblivion."

-Sir Henry Maximilian Beerbohm, 1872-1956

"Philosophy: A route of many roads leading form nowhere to nothing."

-Ambrose Gwinnett Bierce, 1842-1914

"How many people become abstract as a way of appearing profound!"

-Ascribed to Joseph Joubert, 1754-1824

"The fruits of philosophy [are the important thing], not the philosophy itself. When we ask the time, we don't want to know how watches are constructed."

-Ascribed to Georg Christoph Lichtenberg, 1742-1799

"Philosophy's center is everywhere and its circumference nowhere."

-Maurice Merleau-Ponty, 1908-1961

"To ridicule philosophy is really to philosophize."

-Blaise Pascal, 1623-1662

"Religion is a man using a divining rod. Philosophy is a man using a pick and shovel."

-Anonymous

Poetry

See also: Art, Literature, Writing

"Immature poets imitate; mature poets steal."

-Thomas Stearns Eliot, 1888-1965

"I would as soon write free verse as play tennis with the net down."

-Robert Lee Frost, 1874-1963

"No poems can please for long or live that are written by water-drinkers."

-Horace [Quintus Horatius Flaccus], 65-8 B.C.

"Music begins to atrophy when it departs too far from the dance...poetry begins to atrophy when it gets to far from the music."

-Ezra Pound, 1885-1972

"The few bad poems which occasionally are created during abstinence are of no great interest."

-Wilhelm Reich, 1897-1959

"A poem is never finished, only abandoned."

-Ambroise-Paul-Toussaint-Jules Valéry, 1871-1945

Politics

See also: Government, Leadership, Power

"We hang the petty thieves and appoint the great ones to public office."

-*Ascribed to* Aesop, c. 620-550 B.C.

"Nothing doth more hurt in a state than that cunning men pass for wise."

-Sir Francis Bacon, 1561-1626

"The world of politics is always twenty years behind the world of thought."

-John Jay Chapman, 1862-1933

"A liberal is a man who will give away everything he doesn't own."

-*Ascribed to* Frank Dane

"Whenever a man has cast a longing eye on offices, a rottenness begins in his conduct."

-Thomas Jefferson, 1743-1826

"Let us never negotiate out of fear, but let us never fear to negotiate."

-John Fitzgerald Kennedy, 1917-1963

"In politics stupidity is not a handicap."

-Ascribed to Napoléon I [Napoléon Bonaparte], 1769-1821

"They are wrong who think that politics is like an ocean voyage or military campaign, something to be done with some particular end in view."

-Ascribed to Plutarch [Mestrius Plutarchus], 46-127

"Politicians neither love nor hate. Interest, not sentiment, directs them."

-Philip Dormer Stanhope, 4th Earl of Chesterfield, 1694-1774

"The oldest, wisest politician grows not more human so, but is merely a gray wharf rat at last."

-Henry David Thoreau, 1817-1862

"There is a holy mistaken zeal in politics as well as in religion. By persuading others, we convince ourselves."

-The Letters of Junius, 1769-1771

Power

See also: Leadership, Government, Politics

"Mountains defend nothing but themselves."

-Partha Sarathi Bose

"Power tends to corrupt, and absolute power corrupts absolutely."

-John Emerich Edward Dalberg, 1st Baron Acton, 1834-1902

"Power corrupts the few, while weakness corrupts the many."

-Eric Hoffer, 1902-1983

"Nearly all men can stand adversity, but if you want to test a man's character, give him power."

-Ascribed to Abraham Lincoln, 1809-1865

"Whoever is the cause of another becoming powerful is ruined himself."

-Niccolò Machiavelli, 1469-1527

"Right only exists in the small things of civil life. The great things are the dominion of force, cunning, and trickery, and with them religious and moral principles have no influence on the ends or the means."

-August Reichensperger, 1808-1895

"Power does not corrupt men; fools however, if they get into a position of power, corrupt power."

-George Bernard Shaw, 1856-1950

"Human beings cling to their delicious tyrannies and to their exquisite nonsense, like a drunkard to his bottle, and go on till death stares them in the face."

-Sydney Smith, 1771-1845

Praise

See also: Admiration, Fame, Flattery, Gratitude, Respect

"Praise undeserved is satire in disguise."

-Henry Broadhurst, 1840-1911

"To refuse praise reveals a desire to be praised twice over."

-François VI, Duc de La Rochefoucauld, 1613-1680

"Usually we praise only to be praised."

-François VI, Duc de La Rochefoucauld, 1613-1680

"Generally those who boast most of contentment have least of it. Their very boasting shows that they want something, and basely beg it, namely, commendation."

-Thomas Fuller, 1608-1661

"Sometimes we deny being worthy of praise, hoping to generate an argument we would be pleased to lose."

-Cullen Hightower, 1923-

"He who praises everybody praises nobody."

-Dr. Samuel Johnson, 1709-1784

"Never praise a sister to a sister, in the hope of your compliments reaching the proper ears."

-Joseph Rudyard Kipling, 1865-1936

"To exaggerate is to weaken."

-Jean-François de La Harpe

"He is not praised whose praiser deserveth not praise."

-Richard Lichfield, ?-1630

"What men prize most is privilege, even if it be that of chief mourner at a funeral."

-James Russell Lowell, 1819-1891

"He who praises you for what you lack wishes to take from you what you have."

-Don Juan Manuel, Duque de Peñafiel , 1282-1349

"So long as men praise you, you can only be sure that you are not yet on your own path but on someone else's."

-Friedrich Wilhelm Nietzsche, 1844-1900

"We bestow on others praise in which we do not believe, on condition that in return they bestow upon us praise in which we do."

-Jean Rostand, 1894-1977

"We find it easy to believe that praise is sincere: Why should anyone lie in telling us the truth?"

-Jean Rostand, 1894-1977

"Modesty is the only bait when you angle for praise."

-Philip Dormer Stanhope, 4th Earl of Chesterfield, 1694-1773

"When a proud man hears another praised, he feels himself injured."

-English proverb

"A man seldom gives praise gratis. He commends a qualification in another, but then he would be thought himself to be a master of that qualification."

-Anonymous

Prejudice

See also: Hatred, Judgment, Justice

"Intolerance is natural and logical, for in every dissenting opinion lies an assumption of superior wisdom."

-Ambrose Gwinnett Bierce, 1842-1914

"The people who are most bigoted are the people who have no conviction at all."

-Gilbert Keith Chesterton, 1874-1936

"I have seen gross intolerance shown in support of tolerance."

-Samuel Taylor Coleridge, 1772-1834

"As in political, so in literary action, a man wins friends for himself mostly by the passion of his prejudices."

-Joseph Conrad, 1857-1924

"Fortunately for serious minds, a bias recognized is a bias sterilized."

-Albert Eustace Haydon, 1880-1975

"Prejudice is the child of ignorance."

-William Hazlitt, 1778-1830

"Without the aid of prejudice and custom, I should not be able to find my way across the room."

-William Hazlitt, 1778-1830

"Nobody outside of a baby carriage or a judge's chamber believes in an unprejudiced point of view."

-*Ascribed to* Lillian Florence Hellman, 1905-1984

"The mind of a bigot is like the pupil of the eye; the more light you pour upon it, the more it will contract."

-*Ascribed to* Oliver Wendell Holmes, Jun., 1841-1935

"Never look down on anybody unless you're helping them up."

-*Ascribed to* Jesse Louis Jackson, Sen., 1941-

"Everyone is a prisoner of his own experiences. No one can eliminate prejudices—just recognize them."

-Edward Roscoe Murrow, 1908-1965

"Prejudice is a sin everyone denounces and almost no one seriously confesses."

-Ralph Washington Sockman, 1889-1970

"We are always paid for our suspicion by finding what we suspect."

-Henry David Thoreau, 1817-1862

"Passion and prejudice govern the world; only under the name of reason."

-John Wesley, 1703-1791

Pride

See also Praise, Respect

"When science discovers the center of the universe, a lot of people will be disappointed to find they are not it."

-*Ascribed to* Bernard Baily, 1816-1902

"Monkeys are superior to men in this: When a monkey looks into a mirror, he sees a monkey."

-Malcolm de Chazal, 1902-1981

"It is always the secure who are humble."

-Gilbert Keith Chesterton, 1874-1936

"Though pride is not a virtue, it is the parent of many virtues."

-John Churton Collins, 1848-1908

"Mediocrity requires aloofness to preserve its dignity."

-Charles Gates Dawes, 1865-1951

"Every man has a right to be conceited until he is successful."

-Benjamin Disraeli, Earl of Beaconsfield, 1804-1881

"He was like a cock who thought the sun had risen to hear him crow."

-Geoge Eliot [Marian Evans Cross], 1819-1880

"In a tavern everybody puts on airs except the landlord."

-Ralph Waldo Emerson, 1803-1882

"Take egotism out and you would castrate the benefactors."

-Ralph Waldo Emerson, 1803-1882

"Pride gets no pleasure out of having something; only out of having more of it than the next man...It is the comparison that makes you proud: the pleasure of being above the rest."

-Clive Staples Lewis, 1898-1963

"Modesty and unselfishness—these are virtues which men praise—and pass by."

-André Maurois [Emile Salomon Wilhelm Herzog], 1885-1967

"Pride is generally censured and decried, but mainly by those who have nothing to be proud of."

-Arthur Schopenhauer, 1788-1860

"Humility is a virtue all preach, none practice; and yet everybody is content to hear."

-John Selden, 1584-1654

"Self-love, my liege, is not so vile a sin as self-neglecting."

-William Shakespeare, 1564-1616

"There are no grades of vanity; there are only grades of ability in concealing it."

-Mark Twain [Samuel Langhorne Clemens], 1835-1910

"Pride goeth before destruction, and an haughty spirit before a fall."

-*The Proverbs* 16:18

Progress

See also: Achievement, Experience, Success

"All progress is based upon a universal, innate desire on the part of every organism to live beyond its income."

-Samuel Butler, 1835-1902

"Nothing ever gets anywhere. The earth keeps turning round and gets nowhere. The moment is the only thing that counts."

-Jean Maurice Eugène Clément Cocteau, 1889-1963

"Expansion means complexity, and complexity decay."

-Cyril Northcote Parkinson, 1909-1993

"There is in a man an upwelling spring of life, energy, love, whatever you like to call it. If a course is not cut for it, it turns the ground round it into a swamp."

-Mark Rutherford [William Hale White], 1831-1913

"Progress is impossible without change, and those who cannot change their minds cannot change anything."

-*Ascribed to* George Bernard Shaw, 1856-1950

"A ship in harbor is safe—but that is not what ships are for."

-John Augustus Shedd, 1859-1928

"Growth demands a temporary surrender of security."

-Gail Sheehy, 1937-

"Nothing contributes so much to tranquilize the mind as a steady purpose."

-Mary Wollenstonecraft Shelley, 1797-1851

Promises

See also: Deception, Lies, Trust, Truth

"Oaths are but words, and words but wind."

-Samuel Butler, 1612-1680

"Vows begin when hope dies."

-Leonardo di ser Piero da Vinci, 1452-1519

"Treaties are like roses and young girls—they last while they last."

-Charles André Joseph Marie de Gaulle, 1890-1970

"Word and deed are two different things."

-Fyodor Mikhailovich Dostoevsky

"Unless commitment is made, there are only promises and hopes; but no plans."

-Peter Ferdinand Drucker, 1905-2005

"The best way to keep one's word is not to give it."

-Napoléon I [Napoléon Bonaparte], 1769-1821

"He who is slowest in making a promise is most faithful in its performance."

-Jean-Jacques Rousseau, 1712-1778

"Men's vows are women's traitors."

-William Shakespeare, 1564-1616

"The vow that binds too strictly snaps itself."

-Alfred Tennyson, 1st Baron Tennyson 1809-1892

"He loses his thanks who promises and delays."

-Anonymous

Quotations

See also Wit, Writing

"Constant popping off of proverbs will make thee a byword thyself."

-Thomas Fuller, 1608-1661

"A proverb is one man's wit and all men's wisdom."

-Bertrand Arthur William Russell, 3rd Earl of Russell, 1872-1970

"A short saying oft contains much wisdom."

-Sophocles, 496-406 B.C.

"The nicest thing about quotes is that they give us a nodding acquaintance with the originator which is often socially impressive."

-Kenneth Williams, 1926-1988

"Some for renown, on scraps of learning dote, and think they grow immortal as they quote."

-Edward Young, 1683-1765

Reasoning

See also Beliefs, Thought

"Logic and consistency are luxuries for the gods and the lower animals, only."

-Samuel Butler, 1835-1902

"Reason is passion's slave."

-Fyodor Mikhailovich Dostoevsky, 1821-1881

"Common sense is the collection of prejudices acquired by age eighteen."

-Albert Einstein, 1879-1955

"Nothing has an uglier look to us than reason, when it is not on our side."

-George Savile, 1st Marquess of Halifax, 1633-1695

"The man who listens to reason is lost: Reason enslaves all whose minds are not strong enough to master her."

-George Bernard Shaw, 1856-1950

"Man is a reasonable animal who always loses his temper when he is called upon to act in accordance with the dictates of reason."

-Oscar Fingal O'Flahertie Wilde, 1854-1900

Regrets

See also Sadness

"A stiff apology is a second insult."

-Gilbert Keith Chesterton, 1874-1936

"Our repentance is not so much regret for the ill we have done as fear of the ill that may happen to us in consequence."

-François VI, Duc da Le Rochefoucauld, 1613-1680

"The follies which a man regrets most are those which he didn't commit when he had the opportunity."

-Helen Rowland, 1875-1950

"Keep off your thoughts from things that are past and done; for thinking of the past wakes regret and pain."

-Arthur Waley, 1889-1966

"It is a good rule in life never to apologize. The right sort of people do not want apologies, and the wrong sort take a mean advantage of them."

-Sir Pelham Grenville Wodehouse, 1881-1975

Relationships

See also: Family, Humanity, Love, Men, Women

"Men who do not make advances to women are apt to become victims to women who make advances to them."

-Walter Bagehot, 1826-1877

"The big difference between sex for money and sex for free is that sex for money usually costs a lot less."

-*Ascribed to* Brendan Francis Behan, 1923-1964

"What a woman says to her ardent lover should be written in wind and running water."

-Galius Valerius Catullus, 87-54 B.C.

"Between cultivated minds the first interview is the best."

-Ralph Waldo Emerson, 1803-1882

"Solitude, the safeguard of mediocrity, is to genius the stern friend."

-Ralph Waldo Emerson, 1803-1882

"We often irritate others when we think we could not possible do so."

-François VI, Duc de La Rochefoucauld, 1613-1680

"A man would create another man if one did not already exist, but a woman might live an eternity without even thinking of reproducing her own sex."

-Johann Wolfgang von Goethe, 1749-1834

"It is because of men that women dislike one another."

-Jean de La Bruyère, 1645-1695

"A kiss can be a comma, a question mark, or an exclamation point. That's a basic spelling that every woman should know."

-Mistinguett [Jeanne Bourgeois], 1874-1956

"I, myself, alone, and that suffices"

-Napoléon I [Napoléon Bonaparte], 1769-1821

"Scratch a lover and find a foe."

-Dorothy Parker, 1893-1967

"Woman gives herself as a prize to the weak and as a prop to the strong; and no man ever has what he should."

-Cesare Pavese, 1908-1950

"I present myself to you in a form suitable to the relationship I wish to achieve with you."

-Luigi Pirandello, 1867-1936

"It is seldom indeed that one parts on good terms, because if one were on good terms one would not part."

-Valentin Louis Georges Eugène Marcel Proust, 1871-1922

"Men that cannot entertain themselves want somebody, though they care for nobody."

-George Savile, 1st Marquess of Halifax, 1633-1695

"Scoundrels are always sociable."

-Arthur Schopenhauer, 1788-1860

"Home life as we understand it is no more natural to us than a cage is natural to a cockatoo."

-George Bernard Shaw, 1856-1950

"A man is blind to a thousand minute circumstances which call forth a woman's sedulous attention."

-Mary Wollstonecraft Shelley, 1797-1851

"Where is the good in goodbye?"

-Robert Meredith Willson, 1902-1984

"A relationship is what happens between two people who are waiting for something better to come along."

-Anonymous

Religion

See also Beliefs, Faith

"Christianity is the enemy of liberty and civilization."

-August Ferdinand Bebel, 1840-1913

"He is a self-made man and worships his creator."

-John Bright, 1811-1889

"In all times...particularly in countries torn by religious strife, there are always fanatics who ask for nothing better than to become martyrs."

-Alexandre Dumas, Père [Dumas Davy de la Pailleterie], 1802-1870

"A fanatic is a man who does what he thinks the Lord would do if He knew the facts of the case."

-Finely Peter Dunne, 1865-1936

"Science without religion is lame; religion without science is blind."

-Albert Einstein, 1879-1955

"Avoid, as you would the plague, a clergyman who is also a man of business."

-Saint Jerome, 342-420

"Prayer does not change God, but it changes him who prays."

-Søren Aabye Kierkegaard, 1813-1855

"A pious man is one who would be an atheist if the king were."

-Jean de La Bruyère, 1645-1695

"To what excesses will men not go for the sake of a religion in which they believe so little and which they practice so imperfectly!"

-Jean de La Bruyère, 1654-1695

"Every sect is a moral check on its neighbor. Competition is as wholesome in religion as in commerce."

-Walter Savage Landor, 1775-1864

"There are few men who durst publish to the world the prayers they make to the almighty God."

-Michel Eyquem de Montaigne, 1533-1592

"Religion is excellent stuff for keeping the common people quiet."

-*Ascribed to* Napoléon I [Napoléon Bonaparte], 1769-1821

"Religion is what keeps the poor man from murdering the rich."

-*Ascribed to* Napoléon I [Napoléon Bonaparte], 1769-1821

"I never knew any man in my life who could not bear another's misfortunes perfectly like a Christian."

-Alexander Pope, 1688-1744

"Most men's anger about religion is as if two men should quarrel for a lady that neither of them care for."

-George Savile, 1st Marquess of Halifax, 1633-1695

"We have just enough religion to make us hate, but not enough to make us love one another."

-Jonathan Swift, 1667-1745

"The radical invents the views. When he has worn them out, the conservative adopts them."

-Mark Twain [Samuel Langhorne Clemens], 1835-1910

"Spirituality is not religion, religion divides people; belief in something unites them."

-From the Motion Picture *Flight of the Phoenix*, 2004

"What men usually ask of God when they pray is that two and two not make four."

-Anonymous

Respect

See also: Admiration, Faith, Fame, Glory, Praise

"We submit to the majority because we have to. But we are not compelled to call our attitude of subjection a posture of respect."

-Ambrose Gwinnett Bierce, 1842-1914

"It is better to be respected than it is to be popular. Popularity ends on yearbook day, but respect lasts forever."

-John Bytheway, 1962-

"We are less hurt by the contempt of fools than by the lukewarm approval of men of intelligence."

-Luc de Clapiers, Marquis de Vauvenargues, 1715-1747

"No person was ever honored for what he received. Honor has been the reward for what he gave."

-Calvin Coolidge, 1872-1933

"So often, in our quest to be more popular and to be part of the 'in group', we lose sight of things that are far more important."

-Dr. Stephen Richards Covey, 1932-2012

"The louder he talked on his honor, the faster we counted our spoons."

-Ralph Waldo Emerson, 1803-1882

"Take care how thou offendest men raised from low condition."

-Dr. Thomas Fuller, 1654-1734

"Be kind to nerds, you may someday be working for one."

-*Ascribed to* William "Bill" Henry Gates III, 1955-

"When everyone is against you, it means that you are absolutely wrong—or absolutely right."

-*Ascribed to* Albert Guinon, 1863-1923

"Acceptance, it is the true thing everyone longs for."

-*Ascribed to* Rena Harmon

"Popularity? It is glory's small change."

-Victor Marie Hugo, 1802-1885

"As soon as we attract enough attention in the world to play a part in it, we are set rolling like a ball which will never again be at rest."

-Charles Joseph Lamoral, 7te Fürst von Ligne, 1735-1814

"The art of acceptance is the art of making someone who has just done you a small favor wish that he might have done you a greater one."

-*Ascribed to* Joseph Russell Lynes, Jun., 1910-1991

"No one is more dangerous than the one who has been humiliated."

-Nelson Rolihlahla Mandela, 1918-

"No man of honor ever quite lives up to his code, any more than a moral man manages to avoid sin."

-Henry Louis Mencken, 1880-1956

"There are no perfectly honorable men; but every true man has one main point of honor and a few minor ones."

-George Bernard Shaw, 1856-1950

"When people do not respect us we are sharply offended; yet deep down in his heart no man much respects himself."

-Mark Twain [Samuel Langhorne Clemens], 1835-1910

Sadness

See also Happiness

"Wisdom comes alone through suffering."

-Aeschylus, 525-456 B.C.

"This miserable state is borne by the wretched souls of those who lived without disgrace and without praise."

-Dante Alighieri, 1265-1321

"Unhappiness is best defined as the difference between our talents and our expectations."

-Dr. Edward de Bono, 1933-

"For broad understanding and deep feeling, you need pain and suffering...really great men must experience great sadness in the world."

-Fyodor Mikhailovich Dostoevsky, 1821-1881

"The chief mourner does not always attend the funeral."

-Ralph Waldo Emerson, 1803-1882

"Waste not fresh tears over old grief's."

-Euripides, 485-406 B.C.

"Solemnity is a device of the body to hide the faults of the mind."

-François VI, Duc de La Rochefoucauld, 1613-1680

"If you are still being hurt by an event that happened to you at twelve, it is the thought that is hurting you now."

-*Ascribed to* James Hillman, 1926-2011

"Those who do not feel pain seldom think that it is felt."

-Dr. Samuel Johnson, 1709-1784

"While grief is fresh, every attempt to divert it only irritates."

-Dr. Samuel Johnson, 1709-1784

"Happiness is beneficial for the body, but it is grief that develops the powers of the mind."

-Valentin Louis Georges Eugène Marcel Proust, 1871-1922

"Man is the only animal who causes pain to others with no other object than wanting to do so."

-Arthur Schopenhauer, 1788-1860

"Solemnity is the shield of idiots."

-Charles-Louis de Secondat, Baron de La Brède et de Montesquieu, 1689-1750

"It requires more courage to suffer than to die."

-Lucius Annaeus Seneca, c. 4 B.C.-65

"Misery acquaints a man with strange bedfellows."

-William Shakespeare, 1564-1616

"To weep is to make less the depth of grief."

-William Shakespeare, 1564-1616

"When sorrows come, they come not as single spies, but in battalions."

-William Shakespeare, 1564-1616

"Excessive sorrow prevents improvement or enjoyment, or even the discharge of daily usefulness, without which no man is fit for society."

-Mary Wollstonecraft Shelley, 1797-1851

"There are few sorrows, however poignant, in which a good income is of no avail."

-Logan Pearsall Smith, 1865-1946

"The greatest griefs are those we cause ourselves."

-Sophocles, c. 496-406 B.C.

"The keenest sorrow is to recognize ourselves as the sole cause of all our adversities."

-Sophocles, c. 496-406 B.C.

"Your sorrows are the bricks and mortar of a magnificent temple. What you are today and what you will be tomorrow are because of what you have been."

-*Ascribed to* Gordon Wright, 1912-2000

"The deeper the sorrow the less tongue is hath."

-The *Talmud*

"Depression is merely anger without enthusiasm."

-Anonymous

Sanity

See also Intelligence, Wisdom

"In things pertaining to enthusiasm, no man is sane who does not know how to be insane on proper occasions."

-Henry Ward Beecher, 1813-1887

"There is but an inch of difference between the cushioned chamber and the padded cell."

-Gilbert Keith Chesterton, 1874-1936

"Insanity is often the logic of an accurate mind over-tasked."

-Oliver Wendell Holmes, Sen., 1806-1894

"Though this be madness, yet there is method in't."

-William Shakespeare, 1564-1616

"A man who is 'of sound mind' is one who keeps the inner madman under lock and key."

-Ambroise-Paul-Toussaint-Jules Valéry, 1871-1945

"Madness is to think of too many things in succession too fast, or of one thing too exclusively."

-*Ascribed to* Voltaire [François Marie Arouet], 1694-1778

Science

See also: Art, Knowledge, Wisdom

"In science, the credit goes to the man who convinces the world, not to the man to whom the idea first occurs."

-Sir Francis "Frank" Darwin, 1848-1925

"Technology is a wonderful servant, but a horrible master."

-Elizabeth Patterson

"Mathematics is the only science where one never knows what one is talking about nor whether what is said to be true."

-Bertrand Arthur William Russell, 3rd Earl of Russell, 1872-1970

"None but those who have experienced them can conceive of the enticements of science."

-Mary Wollstonecraft Shelley, 1797-1851

Secrecy

See also: Deception, Lies, Trust, Truth

"Anything will give up its secrets if you love it enough."

-George Washington Carver, 1864-1943

"Secrets with girls, like loaded guns with boys,
Are never valued till they make a noise"

-George Crabbe, 1754-1832

"The best way to find out if a man has done something is to advise him to do it. He will not be able to resist boasting that he has done it without being advised."

-Comtesse Diane [Marie Josephine de Suin de Beausacq], 1829-1899

"You can take better care of your secret than another can."

-Ralph Waldo Emerson, 1803-1882

"Three may keep a secret, if two of them are dead."

-Dr. Benjamin Franklin, 1706-1790

"If you want to keep something concealed from your enemy, do not disclose it to your friend."

-*Ascribed to* Solomon ben Yehuda ibn Gabirol, 1022-1070

"A man keeps another's secret better than he does his own. A woman, on the other hand, keeps her own better than another's."

-Jean de La Bruyère, 1645-1695

"Trust not him with your secrets, who, when left alone in your room, turns over your papers."

-Johann Kaspar Lavater, 1741-1801

"What was silent in the father speaks in the son, and often I found in the son the unveiled secret of the father."

-Friedrich Wilhelm Nietzsche, 1844-1900

"If all persons knew what they said of each other, there would not be four friends in the world."

-Blaise Pascal, 1623-1662

"Nobody will keep the thing he hears to himself, and nobody will repeat just what he hears and no more."

-Lucius Annaeus Seneca, c. 4 B.C.-65

"There are some occasions when a man must tell half his secret, in order to conceal the rest."

-Philip Dormer Stanhope, 4th Earl of Chesterfield, 1694-1773

"A secret may be sometimes best kept by keeping the secret of its being a secret."

-Sir Henry Taylor, 1800-1886

"Nothing is easier than to keep a secret: There needs no more but to shut one's mouth."

-Anonymous

Sin

See also: Deception, God(s), Lies, Religion, Vice

"Saint, *noun*. A dead sinner revised and edited."

-Ambrose Gwinnett Bierce, 1842-1914

"It is mush easier to repent of sins that we have committed than to repent of those we intend to commit."

-Josh Billings [Henry Wheeler Shaw], 1818-1885

"Every blessing ignored becomes a curse."

-Paulo Coelho, 1947-

"That which we call sin in others is experiment for us."

-Ralph Waldo Emerson, 1803-1882

"A busy sinner is a tired saint."

-Brogan Lee Fullmer, 1988-

"If we almost keep the commandments, we almost receive the blessings."

-Bruce Clark Hafen, 1940-

"Men are punished by their sins, not for them."

-Elbert Green Hubbard, 1856-1915

"The boy learns not to fear sin, but the punishment for it; and thus he learns to lie."

-Charles Kingsley, 1819-1875

"Few love to hear the sins they love to act."

-William Shakespeare, 1564-1616

"Nothing emboldens sin so much as mercy."

-William Shakespeare, 1564-1616

"Personal sin reflected upon breeds compassion."

-John M. Shanahan, 1939-

"Women keep a special corner of their hearts for sins they have never committed."

-*Ascribed to* Cornelia Otis Skinner, 1901-1979

"The only difference between the saint and the sinner is that every saint has a past, and every sinner has a future."

-Oscar Fingal O'Flahertie Wilde, 1854-1900

Society

See also: Children, Humanity, Men, Parents, Relationships, Women

"What do we live, but to make sport for our neighbors, and laugh at them in turn?"

-Jane Austen, 1775-1817

"It is bad to be oppressed by a minority, but it is worse to be oppressed by a majority. For there is a reserve of latent power in the masses, which if it is called into play, the minority can seldom resist. But from the absolute will of an entire people there is no appeal, no redemption, no refuge but treason."

-John Emerich Edward Dalberg, 1st Baron Acton, 1834-1902

"The best things and best people rise out of their separateness; I'm against a homogenized society because I want the cream to rise."

-Robert Lee Frost, 1874-1963

"The minority is always right."

-Henrick Johan Ibsen, 1828-1906

"Our civilization is founded on the shambles, and every individual existence goes out in a lonely spasm of helpless agony."

-William James, 1842-1910

"There are people whom one should like very well to drop, but would not wish to be dropped by."

-Dr. Samuel Johnson, 1709-1784

"People are there to be there."

-Tyson Robert Skeen, 1986-

"The path of social advancement is, and must be, strewn with broken friendships."

-Herbert George Wells, 1866-1946

"The multitude is always in the wrong."

-Dillion Wentworth, 4th Earl of Rosscommon, 1633-1685

"The worst form of tyranny the world has ever known: the tyranny of the weak over the strong. It is the only tyranny that lasts."

-Oscar Fingal O'Flahertie Wilde, 1854-1900

"Everybody is somebody else's weirdo."

-Dilbert's Rules of Order

"Beware of the tyranny of the minority."

-Latin proverb

"He who builds on the people builds on mud."

-Trite proverb

Sport(s)

See also Interests

"Though boys throw stones at frogs in sport, the frogs do not die in sport, but in earnest."

-Bion, c. 325- c. 255 B.C.

"Push yourself again and again. Don't give an inch until the final buzzer sounds."

-Larry Joe Bird, 1956-

"Sports do not build character. They reveal it."

-Heywood Broun, 1888-1939

"A team effort is a lot of people doing what I say."

-Robert Michael Winner, 1935-2013

"Individuals play the game, but teams win championships."

-Anonymous

Strength

See also Power

"It is the destiny of the weak to be devoured by the strong."

-Otto von Bismarck, 1st Herzog von Lauenburg, 1st Graf von Bismarck-Schönhausen,
1st Fürst von Bismarck
1815-1898

"If you're strong enough, there are no precedents."

-Francis Scott Key Fitzgerald, 1896-1940

"Weak people never give way when they ought to."

-Jean François-Paul de Gondi, Cardinal de Retz, 1614-1679

"One sword keeps another in the sheath."

-George Herbert, 1593-1633

"Rudeness is the weak man's imitation of strength."

-Eric Hoffer, 1902-1983

"It's going to be fun to watch and see how long the meek can keep the earth after they inherit it."

-*Ascribed to* Frank McKinney "Kin" Hubbard, 1868-1930

"At times, our strengths propel us so far forward we can no longer endure our weaknesses and perish from them."

-Friedrich Wilhelm Nietzsche, 1844-1900

"Mediocrity is a hand-rail."

-Charles-Louis de Secondat, Baron de La Brède et de Montesquieu, 1689-1750

"When a man speaks of his strength, he whispers his weakness."

-John M. Shanahan, 1939-

"Pain is weakness leaving the body."

-Anonymous

Substance Abuse

See also Vice

"First you take a drink, then the drink takes a drink, then the drink takes you."

-Francis Scott Key Fitzgerald, 1896-1940

"Drink not the third glass, which thou canst not tame when once it is within thee."

-George Herbert, 1593-1633

"A man who exposes himself when he is intoxicated has not the art of getting drunk."

-Dr. Samuel Johnson, 1709-1784

"Those that merely talk and never think
that live in the wild anarchy of drink."

-Ben Jonson, 1573-1637

"Man, being responsible, must get drunk; the best of life is but intoxication."

-George Gordon Noel, 6th Baron Byron, 1788-1824

"They always talk who never think."

-Matthew Prior, 1664-1721

"When the wine goes in, strange things come out."

-Johann Christoph Friedrich von Schiller, 1775-1854

"'Tis not the drinking that is to be blamed, but the excess."

-John Selden, 1584-1654

"There are two things that will be believed of any man whatsoever, and one of them is that he has taken to drink."

-Newton Booth Tarkington, 1869-1946

"The worst thing about some men is that when they are not drunk they are sober."

-*Ascribed to* William Butler Yeats, 1865-1939

"What is said when drunk has been thought beforehand."

-Flemish proverb

"Under a tattered cloak you will generally find a good drinker."

-Spanish proverb

Success

See also: Achievement, Failure, (Mis)Fortune, Perfection, Progress

"Success has made failures of many men."

-Cindy Adams

"If you live long enough, you'll see that every victory turns into a defeat."

-Simone de Beauvoir, 1908-1986

"Success: The one unpardonable sin against one's fellows."

-Ambrose Gwinnett Bierce, 1842-1914

"An example of the monkey: The higher it climbs, the more you see of its behind."

-Saint Bonaventure [John of Fidanza], 1217-1274

"A minute's success pays the failure of years."

-Robert Browning, 1812-1889

"To be prepared is half the victory."

-Miguel de Cervantes [Miguel de Cervantes Saavedra], 1547-1616

"One must be a god to be able to tell successes from failures without making a mistake."

-Anton Pavlovich Chekhov, 1860-1904

"As always, victory finds a hundred fathers, but defeat is an orphan."

-Gian Galeazzo Ciano, Conte di Cortellazzo and Buccari, 1903-1944

"Great success is more common than great abilities."

-Luc de Clapiers, Marquis de Vauvenargues, 1715-1747

"Men despise great projects when they do not feel themselves capable of great success."

-Luc de Clapiers, Marquis de Vauvenargues, 1715-1747

"The secret of success in life is known only to those who have not succeeded."

-*Ascribed to* John Churton Collins, 1848-1908

"Success doesn't come to you, you go to it."

-Marva Nettles Collins, 1936-

"The secret of success is constancy of purpose."

-Benjamin Disraeli, Earl of Beaconsfield, 1804-1881

"Before you can win you have to think you are worthy."

-*Ascribed to* Michael Keller Ditka, Jun., 1939-

"Victory is never a substitute for wisdom."

-Albert Léon Guérard, 1880-1959

"He was a self-made man who owed his lack of success to nobody."

-Joseph Heller, 1923-1999

"Everything bows to success, even grammar."

-Victor Marie Hugo, 1802-1885

"There is only one success—to be able to spend your life in your own way."

-Christopher Morley, 1890-1957

"If you wish to be a success in the world, promise everything, deliver nothing."

-*Ascribed to* Napoléon I [Napoléon Bonaparte], 1769-1821

"Success has always been a great liar."

-Friedrich Wilhelm Nietzsche, 1844-1900

"Success is how high you bounce when you hit bottom."

-George Smith Patton, Jun., 1885-1945

"Success is an accident...well placed."

-John M. Shanahan, 1939-

"The secret of all victory lies in the organization of the non-obvious."

-Oswald Arnold Gottfried Spengler, 1880-1936

"We never know, believe me, when we have succeeded best."

-Miguel de Unamuno, 1864-1936

"It is not enough to succeed. Others must fail."

-Eugene Luther Gore Vidal, 1925-2012

"Whenever a friend succeeds, a little something in me dies."

-Eugene Luther Gore Vidal, 1925-2012

"One man's wage rise is another man's price increase."

-James Harold Wilson, Baron of Rievaulx, 1916-1995

"I couldn't wait for success...so I went ahead without it."

-Jonathan Harshman Winters III, 1925-2013

"Success is going from failure to failure without a loss of enthusiasm."

-Anonymous

"Success is not so much what you are, but rather what you appear to be."

-Anonymous

Talent

See also Ability, Genius

"There is no such thing as a great talent without great will-power."

-Honoré de Balzac, 1799-1850

"Everyone has talent at twenty-five. The difficulty is to have it at fifty."

-Edward Degas, 1834-1917

"Mediocrity knows nothing higher than itself, but talent instantly recognizes genius."

-Sir Arthur Conan Doyle, 1859-1930

"Use what talents you posses; the woods would be very silent if no birds sang there except those that sang best."

-Ascribed to Henry van Dyke, 1852-1933

"Talent is commonly developed at the expense of character."

-Ralph Waldo Emerson, 1803-1882

"We don't invent our talents in life but rather we detect them."

-Dr. Victor Emil Frankl, 1905-1997

"When someone who holds nothing but trumps, it is impossible to play cards."

-Ascribed to Christian Friedrich Hebbel, 1813-1863

"Everyone has a talent; what is rare is the courage to follow the talent to the dark place where it leads."

-Erica Jong, 1942-

"We can't take any credit for our talents, it's how we use them that counts."

-Madeleine L'Engle, 1918-2007

"Equality of opportunity is an equal opportunity to prove unequal talents."

-Herbert Louis Samuel, 1st Viscount Samuel, 1870-1916

"A great deal of talent is lost to the world for want of a little courage."

-Sydney Smith, 1771-1845

"In the world a man will often be reputed to be a man of sense, only because he is not a man of talent."

-Sir Henry Taylor, 1800-1886

Talking

See also Listening

"No one means all he says, and yet very few say all they mean, for words are slippery and thought is viscous."

-Henry Brooks Adams, 1838-1918

"The habit of common and continuous speech is a symptom of mental deficiency. It proceeds from not knowing what is going on in other people's minds."

-Walter Bagehot, 1826-1877

"Women prefer to talk in two's, while men prefer to talk in three's."

-Gilbert Keith Chesterton, 1874-1936

"When you have nothing to say, say nothing."

-Charles Caleb Colton, 1780-1832

"To do all the talking and not be willing to listen is a form of greed."

-*Ascribed to* Democritus of Abdera, c. 460- c. 370 B.C.

"Blessed is the man who, having nothing to say, abstains from giving in words evidence of the fact."

-Geoge Eliot [Marian Evans Cross], 1819-1880

"Two may talk, and one may hear, but three cannot take part in a conversation of the most sincere and searching sort."

-Ralph Waldo Emerson, 1803-1882

"Nothing is more despicable than a professional talker who uses his words as a quack uses his remedies."

-François Fénelon [François de Salignac de la Mothe], 1651-1715

"Actions speak louder than words, but it is their still silence which clamors the heart."

-Brogan Lee Fullmer, 1988-

"There are people who, instead of listening to what is being said to them, are already listening to what they are going to say themselves."

-*Ascribed to* Albert Guinon, 1863-1923

"The time to stop talking is when the other person nods his head affirmatively but says nothing."

-Ascribed to Henry Samuel Haskins, 1878-1957

"You lose it if you talk about it."

-Ernest Miller Hemingway, 1899-1961

"Silence propagates itself, and the longer talk has been suspended, the more difficult it is to find anything to say."

-Dr. Samuel Johnson, 1709-1784

"The opposite of talking isn't listening. The opposite of talking is waiting."

-Frances "Fran" Ann Lebowitz, 1950-

"Speech is the small change of silence."

-George Meredith, 1828-1909

"No man is exempt from saying silly things; the mischief is to say them deliberately."

-Michel Eyquem de Montaigne, 1533-1592

"Beware of the conversationalist who adds 'in other words.' He is merely starting afresh."

-Robert Morley, 1890-1957

"The more elaborate our means of communication, the less we communicate."

-Ascribed to Joseph Priestley, 1733-1804

"Most people have to talk so they won't hear."

-Ascribed to May Sarton, 1912-1995

"A fool hath no dialogue within himself; the first thought carried him without the reply of a second."

-George Savile, 1st Marquess of Halifax, 1633-1695

"Most men make little use of their speech than to give evidence against their own understanding."

-George Savile, 1st Marquess of Halifax, 1633-1695

"Talkers are no good doers."

-William Shakespeare, 1564-1616

"It is the dread of something happening, something unknown and dreadful, that makes us do anything to keep the flicker of talk from dying out."

-Logan Pearsall Smith, 1865-1946

"Nothing seems to me so insane as bookish language in conversation."

-*Ascribed to* Stendhal [Marie-Henri Beyle], 1783-1843

"We are more anxious to speak than to be heard."

-Henry David Thoreau, 1817-1862

"She understood how much louder a cock can crow in its own farmyard than elsewhere."

-Anthony Trollope, 1815-1882

"Well-timed silence hath more eloquence than speech."

-Martin Farquhar Tupper, 1810-1889

"It is better to be thought an idiot than to speak and remove all doubt."

-*Ascribed to* Mark Twain [Samuel Langhorne Clemens], 1835-1910

"There is no such thing as conversation. It is an illusion. There are intersecting monologues, that is all."

-Dame Rebecca West [Cicily Maxwell Andrews], 1892-1983

"He that keepeth his mouth keepeth his life: but he that openeth wide his lips shall have destruction."

-*The Proverbs* 13:3

"Listen or thy tongue will keep thee deaf."

-American Indian proverb

"Whoever gossips to you will gossip of you."

-Spanish proverb

"The words you speak today should be soft and tender...for tomorrow you may have to eat them."

-Anonymous

Teaching

See also: Education, Intelligence, Knowledge

"A professor is one who talks in someone's sleep."

-*Ascribed to* Wystan Hugh Auden, 1907-1973

"We all love to instruct, though we can teach only what is not worth knowing."

-Jane Austen, 1775-1817

"The essence of teaching is to make learning contagious, to have one idea spark another."

-Marva Nettles Collins, 1936-

"In a completely rational society...the best of us would aspire to be teachers, and the rest of us would have to settle for something less. The job of passing civilization along from one generation to the next ought to be the highest honor anyone could have."

-Lido Anthony "Lee" Iacocca, 1924-

"The man who has never been flogged has never been taught."

-Menander of Athens, c. 342- c. 292 B.C.

"When one in a position of responsibility resists giving needed instruction, or making needed correction, he is only thinking of himself."

-*Ascribed to* Boyd Kenneth Packer, 1924-

"The vanity of teaching doth oft tempt a man to forget that he is a blockhead."

-George Savile, 1st Marquess of Halifax, 1633-1695

"Age is no better, hardly so well, qualified for an instructor as youth, for it has not profited so much as it has lost."

-Henry David Thoreau, 1817-1862

"Nothing that is worth knowing can be taught."

-Oscar Fingal O'Flahertie Wilde, 1854-1900

"When you teach your son, you teach your son's son."

-The *Talmud*

Terrorism

"The only solution to terrorism is for religious scholars to hold a global summit to agree on the definition of 'holy place.' Once they agree on a definition, it will be easier to mock it into submission."

-Scott Raymond Adams, 1957-

"If killing those who kill our sons is terrorism, then let history be witness that we are terrorists."

-Osama bin Mohammed bin Awad bin Laden, 1957-2011

"Terrorist are picadors and matadors. They prick the bull until it bleeds and is blinded by rage, then they snap the red cape of bloody terror in its face....For the bull has failed to understand that the snapping cape was but a provocation to goad it into attacking and exhausting itself for the kill."

-Patrick Joseph "Pat" Buchanan, 1938-

"Wanton killing of innocent civilians is terrorism, not a war against terrorism."

-Avram Noam Chomsky, 1928-

"Any power must be an enemy of mankind which enslaves the individual by terror or force"

-Albert Einstein, 1879-1955

"There's nothing like a stable society to fight terrorism."

-John Dennis Hastert, 1942-

"Terrorism is the tactic of demanding the impossible, and demanding it at gunpoint."

-Christopher Eric Hitchens, 1949-2011

"A 'war against terrorism' is an impracticable conception if it means fighting terrorism with terrorism."

-Sir John Clifford Mortimer, 1923-2009

"If we like them, they're freedom fighters....If we don't like them, they're terrorists. In the unlikely case we can't make up our minds, they're temporarily only guerrillas."

-Carl Edward Sagan, 1934-1996

"How much common sense does it take to know that you cannot end terrorism by indiscriminately dropping bombs?

-Howard Zinn, 1922-2010

Thoughts

See also Ideas

"Analysis kills spontaneity. The grain once ground into flour springs and germinates no more."

-Henri Frédéric Amiel, 1821-1881

"A conclusion is the place where you got tired of thinking."

-Arthur McBride Bloch, 1938-

"People are governed by the head; a kind heart is of little value in chess."

-Sebastien Roch Nicolas Chamfort, 1741-1794

"Dogma does not mean the absence of thought, but the end of thought."

-Gilbert Keith Chesterton, 1874-1936

"A man thinks as he can, not as he will."

-Alexandre Dumas, Père [Dumas Davy de la Pailleterie], 1802-1870

"All my best thoughts were stolen by the ancients."

-Ralph Waldo Emerson, 1803-1882

"In every work of genius, we recognize our own rejected thoughts; they come back to us with a certain alienated majesty."

-Ralph Waldo Emerson, 1803-1882

"How can I tell what I think till I see what I say?"

-Edward Morgan Forster, 1879-1970

"All intelligent thoughts have already been thought; what is necessary is only to try to think them again."

-Johann Wolfgang von Goethe, 1749-1834

"Most of one's life...is one prolonged effort to prevent oneself thinking."

-Aldous Leonard Huxley, 1894-1963

"Almost all rich veins of original and striking speculation have been opened by systematic half-thinkers."

-John Stuart Mill, 1806-1873

"Look wise, say nothing, and grunt. Speech was given to conceal thought."

-Sir William Osler, 1st Baronet Osler, 1849-1919

"Who reflects too much will accomplish little."

-Johann Christoph Friedrich von Schiller, 1775-1854

"Our most important thoughts are those which contradict our emotions."

-*Ascribed to* Ambroise-Paul-Toussaint-Jules Valéry, 1871-1945

"Men use thought only to justify their wrongdoings, and speech only to conceal their thoughts."

-Voltaire [François Marie Arouet], 1694-1778

Time

See also History

"Old age lives minutes slowly, hours quickly; childhood chews hours and swallows minutes."

-*Ascribed to* Malcolm de Chazal, 1902-1981

"A man who dares to waste one hour of time has not discovered the value of life."

-Charles Robert Darwin, 1809–1882

"I am long on ideas, but short on time, I expect to live to be only about a hundred."

-Thomas Alva Edison, 1847-1931

"Dost thou love life? Then do not squander time, for that's the stuff life is made up."

-Dr. Benjamin Franklin, 1706-1790

"Observe due measure, for right timing is in all things the most important factor."

-Hesiod, 700 B.C.

"Things are always at their best in the beginning."

-Blaise Pascal, 1623-1662

"Time is what we want most, but what we use worst."

-William Penn, 1644-1718

"Wait for that wisest of all counselors, time."

-Pericles, 495-429

"Misspending a man's time is a kind of self-homicide."

-George Savile, 1st Marquess of Halifax, 1633-1695

"Come what may, time and hour runs through the roughest day."

-William Shakespeare, 1564-1616

"Deadlines are the mothers of invention."

-John M. Shanahan, 1939-

"You always have a cushion to fall back on when there's time."

-*Ascribed to* John Zacary "Zac" Spencer, 1989-

"There are as many spaces and times as there are subjects."

-Jakob Johann von Uexküll, 1864-1944

"As if you could kill time without injuring eternity."

-Henry David Thoreau, 1817-1862

"Procrastination is the thief of time."

-Edward Young, 1683-1765

Trust

See also: Beliefs, Deception, Faith, Honesty, Lies, Truth

"Trust only movement. Life happens at the level of events, not of words. Trust movement."

-Alfred Adler, 1870-1937

"Trust everyone, but cut the cards."

-Finley Peter Dunne, 1865-1936

"We are much harder on people who betray us in small ways than on people who betray others in great ones."

-François VI, Duc de La Rochefoucauld, 1613-1680

"We are inclined to believe those whom we do not know because they have never deceived us."

-Dr. Samuel Johnson, 1709-1784

"On one issue at least, men and women agree; they both distrust women."

-Henry Louis Mencken, 1880-1956

"What upsets me is not that you lied to me, but that from now on I can no longer believe you."

-Friedrich Wilhelm Nietzsche, 1844-1900

"One has not the right to betray even a traitor. Traitors must be fought, not betrayed."

-Charles "Pierre" Péguy, 1873-1914

"He who mistrusts most should be trusted least."

-*Ascribed to* Theognis, 545 B.C.

"Few things help an individual more than to place responsibility upon him and to let him know what you trust him."

-Booker Taliaferro Washington, 1856-1915

"Treason is a matter of dates."

-From the Motion Picture *The Count of Monte Cristo*, 2002

"It takes years to build up trust, and it only takes suspicion, not proof, to destroy it."

-Anonymous

Truth

See also: Beliefs, Deception, Faith, Honesty, Lies, Trust

"The truth is forced upon us, very quickly, by a foe."

-Aristophanes, 450-385

"Truth is the cry of all, but the game of few."

-George Bishop Berkeley, 1685-1753

"A truth that's told with bad intent beats all the lies you can invent."

-William Blake, 1757-1827

"Nobody speaks the truth when there's something they must have."

-Elizabeth Dorothea Cole Bowen, 1899-1973

"Much truth is spoken, that more may be concealed."

-Sir Charles John Darling, 1st Baron Darling, 1849-1936

"When you have eliminated the impossible, whatever remains, however improbable, must be the truth."

-Sir Arthur Conan Doyle, 1859-1930

"If you leave people without truth, they will make their own."

-Brogan Lee Fullmer, 1988-

"It requires as much caution to tell the truth as to conceal it."

-Baltasar Gracián, 1601-1658

"In human relations kindness and lies are worth a thousand truths."

-Graham Greene, 1904-1991

"What probably distorts everything in life is that one is convinced that one is speaking truth because one says what one thinks."

-Sacha Guitry, 1885-1959

"That Man, who flees from truth, should have invented the mirror is the greatest of historical miracles."

-*Ascribed to* Christian Friedrich Hebbel, 1813-1863

"It is a matter of perfect indifference where a thing originated; the only question is: Is it true in and for itself."

-Georg Wilhelm Friedrich Hegel, 1770-1831

"Truth is a torch that gleams through the fog without dispelling it."

-Claude-Adrien Helvétius, 1715-1771

"Man is ice to truth and fire to falsehood."

-Jean de La Fontaine, 1621-1695

"It is one thing to show a man that he is in an error, and another to put him in possession of the truth."

-John Locke, 1632-1704

"It is hard to believe that a man is telling the truth when you know that you would lie if you were in his place."

-Henry Louis Mencken, 1880-1956

"Give me a fruitful error any time, full of seeds, bursting with its own corrections. You can keep your sterile truth for yourself."

-Vilfredo Federico Damaso Pareto, 1848-1923

"Contradiction is not a sign of falsity, nor the lack of contradiction a sign of truth."

-Blaise Pascal, 1623-1662

"Every truth passes through three stages before it is recognized. In the first, it is ridiculed, in the second it is opposed, in the third it is regarded as self-evident."

-*Ascribed to* Arthur Schopenhauer, 1788-1860

"The closer the truth, the closer to the nerve."

-John M. Shanahan, 1939-

"There are only two ways of telling the complete truth—anonymously and posthumously."

-Ascribed to Thomas Sowell, 1930-

"Truth does not blush."

-Quintus Septimus Tertullianus, 160-240 B.C.

"The thing which has always been accepted by everyone, everywhere, is almost certain to be false."

-Ascribed to Ambroise-Paul-Toussaint-Jules Valéry, 1871-1945

"If you speak the truth, have a foot in the stirrup."

-Turkish proverb

"Truth is the safest lie."

-Yiddish proverb

"Many a truth is spoken in a jest."

-Anonymous

Vengeance

"How right it is to describe vengeance as the pleasure of the gods."

-Alexandre Dumas, Père [Dumas Davy de la Pailleterie], 1802-1870

"Life being what it is, one dreams of revenge."

-Eugène Henri Paul Gauguin, 1848-1903

"Living well is the best revenge."

-George Herbert, 1593-1633

"Your greatest revenge is later their greatest regret."

-Nicole Lynch, 1989-

"Revenge should have no bounds."

-William Shakespeare, 1564-1616

Vice

See also: Evil, Good, Morality, Sin, Virtue

"The vices we scoff at in others, we laugh at within ourselves."

-Sir Thomas Browne, 1605-1682

"Diogenes struck the father when the son swore."

-Robert Burton, 1577-1640

"We are dismayed when we find that even disaster cannot cure us of our faults."

-Luc de Clapiers, Marquess de Vauvenargues, 1715-1747

"If it was necessary to tolerate in other people everything that one permits oneself, life would be unbearable."

-Georges Courteline [Georges-Victor-Marcel Moineau], 1858-1929

"People who have no weaknesses are terrible; there is no way of taking advantage of them."

-Anatole France [Jacques Anatole François Thibault], 1844-1924

"Almost all our faults are more pardonable than the methods we resort to hide them."

-François VI, Duc de La Rochefoucauld, 1613-1680

"If we had no faults of our own, we would not take so much pleasure in noticing those in others."

-François VI, Duc de La Rochefoucauld, 1613-1680

"We confess to little faults only to persuade ourselves that we have no great ones."

-François VI, Duc de La Rochefoucauld, 1613-1680

"When the vices give us up we flatter ourselves that we are giving up them."

-François VI, Duc de La Rochefoucauld, 1613-1680

"If a friend tell thee a fault, imagine always that he telleth thee not the whole."

-Thomas Fuller, 1608-1661

"It is well that there is no one without a fault, for he would not have a friend in the world: he would seem to belong to a different species."

-William Hazlitt, 1778-1830

"It has been my experience that folks who have no vices have very few virtues."

-Abraham Lincoln, 1809-1865

"I prefer an accommodating vice to an obstinate virtue."

-Molière [Jean-Baptiste Poquelin], 1622-1673

"Just as those who practice the same profession recognize each other instinctively, so do those who practice the same vice."

-Valentin Louis Georges Eugène Marcel Proust, 1871-1922

"In our ideals we unwittingly reveal our vices."

-Jean Rostand, 1894-1977

"A wife is to thank God her husband hath faults....A husband without faults is a dangerous observer."

-George Savile, 1st Marquess of Halifax, 1633-1695

"You saw his weakness, and he will never forgive you."

-Johann Christoph Friedrich von Schiller, 1775-1854

"The cause of this effect,
Or rather say, the cause of this defect,
For this effect defective comes by cause."

-William Shakespeare, 1564-1616

"They say best men are molded out of faults, and, for the most, become much more the better for being a little bad."

-William Shakespeare, 1564-1616

"Don't tell your friends their social faults; they will cure the fault and never forgive you."

-Logan Pearsall Smith, 1865-1946

"People hate those who make them feel their own inferiority."

-Philip Dormer Stanhope, 4th Earl of Chesterfield, 1694-1773

"And why beholdest thou the mote that is in thy brothers eye, but considerest not the beam that is in thine own eye?"

-*The Gospel According to Matthew 7:3*

Virtue

See also: Evil, Good, Morality, Sin, Vice

"We are what we repeatedly do. Excellence, then, is not an act, but a habit."

-Aristotle, 384 BC-322 BC

"Make me chaste and content, but not just yet."

-Saint Augustine [Aurelius Augustinus], 354-430

"If we escape punishment for our vices, why should we complain if we are not rewarded for our virtues?"

-John Churton Collins, 1848-1908

"Virtue is praised but hated. People run away from it, for it is ice-cold, and in this world you must keep your feet warm."

-Denis Diderot, 1713-1784

"To many people, virtue consists chiefly in repenting faults, not in avoiding them."

-*Ascribed to* Georg Christoph Lichtenberg, 1742-1799

"The strength of a man's virtue should not be measured by his special exertions, but by his habitual acts."

-Blaise Pascal, 1623-1662

"When men grow virtuous in their old age, they only make a sacrifice to God of the devil's leavings."

-Alexander Pope, 1688-1744

"No one gossips about other people's secret virtues."

-Bertrand Arthur William Russell, 3rd Earl of Russell, 1872-1970

"Our virtues and vices couple with one another, and get children that resemble both their parents."

> -George Savile, 1st Marquess of Halifax, 1633-1695

"Men's evil manners live in brass; their virtues we write in water."

> -William Shakespeare, 1564-1616

"Some rise by sin, and some by virtue fall."

> -William Shakespeare, 1564-1616

"Virtues, like essences, lose their fragrance when exposed."

> -William Shenstone, 1714-1763

"Women's virtue is a man's greatest invention."

> -*Ascribed to* Cornelia Otis Skinner, 1901-1979

War

See also Conflict, Enemies

"The importance of a state is measured by the number of soldiers it can put into the filed of battle."

> -Otto von Bismarck, 1st Herzog von Lauenburg, 1st Graf von Bismarck-Schönhausen,
> 1st Fürst von Bismarck
> 1815-1898

"It is avarice and hatred; it is that quivering lip, that cold, hating eye, which built magazines and powder-houses."

> -Ralph Waldo Emerson, 1803-1882

"War is the result of the sacrifice of many for the actions of few, and the ambitions of the lonely."

> -Brogan Lee Fullmer, 1988-

"The first blow is half the battle."

> -Oliver Goldsmith, 1728-1774

"Every man thinks meanly of himself for not having been a soldier, or not having been to sea."

> -Dr. Samuel Johnson, 1709-1784

"Let him not boast who puts his armor on as he who puts it off, the battle done."

-Henry Wadsworth Longfellow, 1807-1882

"A prince should have no other object or thought in mind than war and how to wage it."

-Niccolò Machiavelli, 1469-1527

"War is an ugly thing, but not the ugliest of things. The decayed and degraded state of moral and patriotic feeling which thinks that nothing is worth war is much worse."

-John Stuart Mill, 1806-1873

"War hath no fury like a non-combatant."

-Charles Edward Montague, 1867-1928

"An army marches on its stomach."

-*Ascribed to* Napoléon I [Napoléon Bonaparte], 1769-1821

"The battle is lost: we have time to win another."

-Napoléon I [Napoléon Bonaparte], 1769-1821

"The whole art of war consists in a well-reasoned and extremely circumspect defensive, followed by rapid and audacious attack."

-*Ascribed to* Napoléon I [Napoléon Bonaparte], 1769-1821

"In war, there are no unwounded soldiers."

-Franses de José Narosky, c. 1930-

"The object of war is peace, and the purposes of peace are mutual good-will and advantageous commercial intercourse."

-John Russell, 1st Earl Russell, 1792-1878

"Farewell the tranquil mind, farewell content,
Farewell the plumèd troops and the big wars
That makes ambition virtue!"

-William Shakespeare, 1564-1616

"'Tis the soldier's life
To have their balmy slumbers waked with strife."

-William Shakespeare, 1564-1616

"A military operation involves deception. Even though you are competent, appear to be incompetent. Though effective, appear to be ineffective."

-Sun-tzu, c. 544-496 B.C.

"Victorious warriors win first and then go to war, while defeated warriors go to war first and then seek to win."

-Sun-tzu, c. 544-496 B.C.

"Nothing except a battle lost can be half so melancholy as a battle won."

-Arthur Wellesley, 1st Duke of Wellington, 1769-1852

Wealth

See also: Achievement, (Mis)Fortune, Success

"Thousands upon thousands are yearly brought into a state of real poverty by their great anxiety not to be thought poor."

-William Andrus Alcott, 1798-1859

"When there is no middle class, and the poor greatly exceed in number, troubles arise, and the state soon comes to an end."

-Aristotle, 384-322 B.C.

"The dearer a thing is, the cheaper as a general rule we sell it."

-Samuel Butler, 1835-1902

"The man who dies rich...dies disgraced."

-Andrew Carnegie, 1835-1919

"Three generations from shirtsleeves to shirtsleeves."

-Andrew Carnegie, 1835-1919

"Ah, if the rich were rich as the poor fancy riches."

-Ralph Waldo Emerson, 1803-1882

"When the well's dry, we know the worth of water."

-Dr. Benjamin Franklin, 1706-1790

"Money is the answer. What is the question?"

-Garlin Larry Fullmer, 1954-

"Poverty sits by the cradle of all our great men and rocks all of them to manhood."

-Christian Johann Heinrich Heine, 1797-1856

"The creditor hath a better memory than the debtor."

-James Howell, 1594-1666

"When a fellow says it hain't the money but the principle o' the thing, it's th' money."

-Frank McKinney "Kin" Hubbard, 1868-1930

"You never find people laboring to convince you that you may live very happily upon a plentiful fortune."

-Dr. Samuel Johnson, 1709-1784

"If a free society cannot help the many who are poor, it cannot save the few who are rich."

-John Fitzgerald Kennedy, 1917-1963

"All affectation is the vain and ridiculous attempt of poverty to appear rich."

-Johann Kaspar Lavater, 1741-1801

"Say not you know another entirely, till you have divided an inheritance with him."

-Johann Kaspar Lavater, 1741-1801

"The value of money is that with it we can tell any man to go to the devil. It is the sixth sense which enables you to enjoy the other five."

-William Somerset Maugham, 1874-1965

"Riches do not consist in the possession of treasures, but in the use made of them."

-Napoléon I [Napoléon Bonaparte], 1769-1821

"Possessions are usually diminished by possession."

-Friedrich Wilhelm Nietzsche, 1844-1900

"Upper classes are a nation's past; the middle class is its future."

-Ayn Rand [Alisa Zinov'yevna Rosenbaum], 1905-1982

"Neither a borrower nor a lender be;
For loan oft loses both itself and friend,
And borrowing dulls the edge of husbandry."

-William Shakespeare, 1564-1616

"Poverty does not produce unhappiness: It produces degradation."

-George Bernard Shaw, 1856-1950

"Every single instance of a friend's insincerity increases our dependence on the efficiency of money."

-William Shenstone, 1714-1763

"Nothing knits man to man like the frequent passage from hand to hand of cash."

-Walter Richard Sickert, 1860-1942

"Let all the learned say what they can,
'Tis ready money makes the man."

-William Somerville, 1675-1742

"No man is rich enough to buy back his past."

-Oscar Fingal O'Flahertie Wilde, 1854-1900

"You can't have everything, where would you put it?"

-Steven Alexander Wright, 1955-

"Wealth gotten by vanity shall be diminished: but he that gathereth by labour shall increase."

-*The Proverbs* 13:11

"The poor is hated even of his own neighbour: but the rich hath many friends."

-*The Proverbs* 14:20

"For the love of money is the root of all evil: which while some coveted after, they have erred from the faith pierced themselves through with many sorrows."

-*First Epistle to Timothy* 6:10

"Before borrowing money from a friend, decide which you need most."

-American proverb

"It is an easy matter for a stingy man to get rich—but what's the use?"

-American proverb

"If you want to know what a man is really like, take notice how he acts when he loses money."

-New England proverb

"A rich man is either a scoundrel or the heir of a scoundrel."

-Spanish proverb

"Rich man down and poor man up—they are still not even."

-Yiddish proverb

"If who I am is what I have and what I have is lost, then who am I?"

-Anonymous

Wisdom

See also: Education, Experience, Genius, Intelligence

"It is a profitable thing, if one is wise, to seem foolish."

-Aeschylus, 525-456 B.C.

"The wise person questions himself, the fool others."

-Henri Arnold, 1918-

"There are more fools than knaves in the world; else the knaves would not have enough to live upon."

-Samuel Butler, 1612-1680

"Never mistake knowledge for wisdom. One helps you make a living; the other helps you make a life."

-Sandra Carey, 1941-

"Wisdom consists of the anticipation of consequences."

-Norman Cousins, 1912-1990

"Who are a little wise, the best fools be."

-John Donne, 1572-1631

"A wise man's questions contain half the answer."

-Solomon ben Yehuda ibn Gabirol, 1022-1070

"Knowledge speaks, but wisdom listens."

-*Ascribed to* James Marshall "Jimi" Hendrix, 1942-1970

"Knowledge can be communicated but not wisdom."

-Herman Hesse, 1877-1962

"The art of being wise is the art of knowing what to overlook."

-William James, 1842-1910

"It's bad taste to be wise all the time, like being at a perpetual funeral."

-David Herbert Lawrence, 1885-1930

"There are people who think that everything one does with a serious face is sensible."

-Georg Christoph Lichtenberg, 1742-1799

"A wise man sees as much as he ought, not as much as he can."

-Michel Eyquem de Montaigne

"Not by age but by capacity is wisdom acquired."

-Titus Maccius Plautus, 254-184 B.C.

"No man is the wiser for his learning; it may administer matter to work in, or objects to work upon, but wit and wisdom are born with a man."

-John Selden, 1584-1654

"The fool doth think he is wise, but the wise man knows himself to be a fool."

-William Shakespeare, 1564-1616

"When we are born, we cry that we are come to this great stage of fools."

-William Shakespeare, 1564-1616

"A wise man will live at least as much within his wit as within his income."

-Philip Dormer Stanhope, 4th Earl of Chesterfield, 1694-1773

"Be wise today; 'tis madness to defer."

-Edward Young, 1683-1765

"The poor man's wisdom is despised and his words are not heard."

-*Ecclesiastes* 9:16

"He that walketh with wise men shall be wise: but a companion of fools shall be destroyed."

-*The Proverbs* 13:20

"A wise man hears one word and understands two."

-Jewish proverb

"Men can acquire knowledge but not wisdom. Some of the greatest fools ever known were learned men."

-Spanish proverb

"A wise man knows everything; a shrewd one, everybody."

-Anonymous

Wit

See also Humor

"Wit makes its own welcome, and levels all distinctions."

-Ralph Waldo Emerson, 1803-1882

"The greatest fault of a penetrating wit is to go beyond the mark."

-François VI, Duc de La Rochefoucauld, 1613-1680

"The height of cleverness is to be able to conceal it."

-François VI, Duc de La Rochefoucauld, 1613-1680

"A man has made great progress in cunning when he does not seem too clever to others."

-Jean de La Bruyère, 1645-1695

"He who doesn't lose his wits over certain things has no wits to lose."

-Gotthold Ephraim Lessing, 1729-1781

"It is not enough to possess wit. One must have enough of it to avoid having too much."

-André Maurois [Emile Salomon Wilhelm Herzog], 1885-1967

"The well of true wit is truth itself."

-George Meredith, 1828-1909

"Wit has truth in it; wisecracking is simply calisthenics with words."

-Dorothy Parker, 1893-1967

"Brevity is the soul of wit."

-William Shakespeare, 1564-1616

"If you want to be witty, work on your character and say what you think on every occasion."

-Stendhal [Marie-Henri Beyle], 1783-1843

"Never engage in a battle of wits with an unarmed person."

-Anonymous

"Wit is far more often a shield than a lance."

-Anonymous

Women

See also: Humanity, Men, Relationships, Society

"Women are never stronger than when they arm themselves with their weakness."

-Madame du Deffand [Marie de Vichy-Chamrond], Marquise de Deffand, 1697-1780

"It is only rarely that one can see in a little boy the promise of a man, but one can almost always see in a little girl the threat of a woman."

-*Ascribed to* Alexandre Dumas, Fils, 1824-1895

"Most men who rail against women are railing at one woman only."

-*Ascribed to* Rémy de Gourmont, 1858-1915

"Every woman is wrong until she cries, and then she is right—instantly."

-*Ascribed to* Thomas Chandler Haliburton], 1796-1865

"The silliest woman can manage a clever man; but it needs a very clever woman to manage a fool!"

-Joseph Rudyard Kipling, 1865-1936

"Women run to extremes; they are either better or worse than men."

-Jean de La Bruyère, 1645-1695

"You don't know a woman until you have had a letter from her."

-Ada Leverson, 1862-1933

"Women do not find it difficult nowadays to behave like men, but they often find it extremely difficult to behave like gentlemen."

-Sir Compton Mackenzie, 1883-1972

"The females of all species are most dangerous when they appear to retreat."

-Donald Robert Perry Marquis, 1878-1937

"You do not need a head, nor even a heart, to be all that a female can require."

-Patrick O'Brian [Richard Patrick Russ], 1914-2000

"Men, some to business, some to pleasure take,
But ev'ry woman is at heart a rake."

-Alexander Pope, 1688-1744

"Frailty thy name is woman."

-William Shakespeare, 1565-1616

"It is assumed that the woman must wait, motionless, until she is wooed. That is how the spider waits for the fly."

-George Bernard Shaw, 1856-1950

"In the eyes of God or biology or what have you, it is just very important to have women."

-*Ascribed to* Norman Tagal

"Women deserve to have more than twelve years between the ages of twenty-eight and forty."

-James Thurber, 1894-1961

"It's a sad house where the hen crows louder than the cock."

-Scottish proverb

"Behind every great man there is a great woman; and behind that woman is his wife."

-Anonymous

"Men who cherish for women the highest respects are seldom popular with them."

-Anonymous

Work

See also Effort

"To do great work, a man must be very idle as well as very industrious."

-Samuel Butler, 1835-1902

"Do not free a camel of the burden of his hump; you may be freeing him from being a camel."

-Gilbert Keith Chesterton, 1874-1936

"Lazy people are always looking for something to do."

-Luc de Clapiers, Marquis de Vauvenargues, 1715-1747

"Far and away, the best prize that life offers is the chance to work hard at work worth doing."

-Theodore Roosevelt, 1858-1919

"I want to be thoroughly used up when I die. For the harder I work the more I live."

-George Bernard Shaw, 1856-1950

"It is better to wear out one's shoes than one's sheets."

-Genoese proverb

"It's always been and always will be the same in the world: The horse does the work and the coachman is tipped."

-Anonymous

Writing

See also: Literature, Poetry

"Devotees of grammatical studies have not been distinguished for any very remarkable felicities of expression."

-Bronson Alcott, 1799-1888

"Chaste men engender obscene literatures."

-Decimus Maximus Ausonius, 310-395

"About the most originality that any writer can hope to achieve honestly is to steal with good judgment."

-Josh Billings [Henry Wheeler Shaw], 1818-1885

"They lard their lean books with the fat of others' works."

-Robert Burton, 1577-1640

"Most editors are failed writers—but so are most writers."

-Thomas Stearns Eliot, 1888-1965

"The chief merit of language is clearness, and we know that nothing detracts so much from this as do unfamiliar terms."

-Galen, 129-199

"The act of writing is the act of discovering what you believe."

-Sir David Hare, 1947-

"No author is a man of genius to his publisher."

-*Ascribed to* Christian Johann Heinrich Heine, 1797-1856

"The most essential gift for a good writer is a built-in, shockproof crap detector. This is the writer's radar and all great writers have had it."

-Ernest Miller Hemingway, 1899-1961

"Only a person with a Best Seller mind can write Best Sellers."

-Aldous Leonard Huxley, 1894-1963

"Language most shows a man; speak that I may see thee."

-Ben Jonson, 1573-1637

"Read over you compositions, and when you meet a passage which you think is particularly fine, strike it out."

-Dr. Samuel Johnson, 1709-1784

"Words, like eyeglasses, blur everything that they do not make more clear."

-Joseph Joubert, 1754-1824

"Words signify a man's refusal to accept the world as it is."

-Walter Arnold Kaufmann, 1921-1980

"A journalist is stimulated by a deadline: He writes worse when he has time."

-Karl Kraus, 1874-1936

"Journalists write because they have nothing to say, and have something to say because they write."

-Karl Kraus, 1874-1936

"We do not write to be understood; we write in order to understand."

-Cecil Day Lewis, 1904-1972

"Freedom of the press is guaranteed only to those who own one."

-Abbott Joseph Liebling, 1904-1963

"Our principle writers have nearly all been fortunate in escaping regular education."

-Hugh MacDiarmid [Christopher Murray Grieve], 1892-1978

"If you steal from one author, it's plagiarism; if you steal from many, it's research."

-Wilson Mizner, 1876-1933

"I have made this letter longer than usual, because I lack the time to make it short."

-Blaise Pascal, 1623-1662

"Just get it down on paper, and then we'll see what to do with it."

-Maxwell Evarts Perkins, 1884-1947

"The original writer is not one who imitates nobody, but one who nobody can imitate."

-François-Auguste René, 1st Vicomte de Chateaubriand, 1768-1848

"A good writer is basically a story-teller, not a scholar or a redeemer of mankind."

-*Ascribed to* Isaac Bashevis Singer, 1904-1991

"What I like in a good author is not what he says, but what he whispers."

-Logan Pearsall Smith, 1865-1946

"It is with words as with sunbeams. The more they are condensed, the deeper they burn."

-Robert Southey, 1774-1843

"As for style of writing, if one has anything to say, it drops from him simply and directly, as a stone falls to the ground."

-Henry David Thoreau, 1817-1862

"How vain it is to sit down to write when you have not stood up to live."

-Henry David Thoreau, 1817-1862

"As to the adjective: When in doubt, strike it out."

-Mark Twain [Samuel Langhorne Clemens], 1835-1910

"The difference between the right word and the almost right word is the difference between lightning and the lightning bug."

-Mark Twain [Samuel Langhorne Clemens], 1835-1910

"Words and sentences are subjects of revision; paragraphs and whole compositions are subjects of prevision."

-Barrett Wendell, 1855-1921

"A man really writes for an audience of about ten persons. Of course if others like it, that is clear gain. But if those ten are satisfied, he is content."

-Alfred North Whitehead, 1861-1947

"The limits of my language mean the limits of my world."

-Ludwig Josef Johann Wittgenstein, 1889-1951

"A synonym is a word you use when you can't spell the other one."

-*Harper's Monthly Magazine*

"Words, like trees, bend with the prevailing winds."

-*Time*

Authors Index

Sources

Adams, Cindy
  Quoted in Joey Adams, *Cindi and I*, 1957, *161*
Adams, Donald Allison
  The Rotarian
    "The Rotary's Idea of Service," page 60, August, 1926, *85*
Adams, Franklin Pierce
  Ballade of Schopenhaur's Philosophy, 1917, *124*
Adams, Henry Brooks
  The Education of Henry Adams, 1907, *23, 165*
Adams, John Quincy
  Ascribed to, *129*
Adams, Scott Raymond
  Dilbert Newsletter, number 58, *169*
Addison, Joseph
  Cato, 1793, act 1, scene 4, *16*
Adler, Alfred
  Sam Walton, 1992, p. 5, *173*
Adler, Mortimer Jerome
  Ascribed to, *110*
Adler, Renata
  "What's So Funny?" *New York Times*, July 7, 1968, *26*
Aeschylus
  Agamemnon, c. 458 B.C., *185*
  Prometheus Bound, c. 458 B.C., *150*
Aesop
  "The Eagle and the Arrow," *The Fables*, c. 550 B.C., *52*
  Ascribed to, *134*
Albright, Herm
  Ascribed to, *14*
Alcott, Bronson
  Talk, Talk, 1868, *191*
Alcott, William Andrus
  The Young Man's Guide, section 15, 1834, *182*
Alda, Alan
  Things I Overheard While Talking to Myself, 2007, *32*
Aldington, Edward Godfree "Richard"
  The Colonel's Daughter: A Novel, 1931, *129*
Ali ibn Abi-Talib
  Quoted in Diogenes Laertius, *Lives of the Philosopher*, *52*
Alighieri, Dante
  Paradiso, canto 1, L. 34, *45*
  The Divine Comedy, Inferno, c. 1321,
    canto 1, Line 32, *85*
    canto 24, Line 77, *150*
American proverb
  Quoted by Adlai Stevenson II in 1951, *107*
Amiel, Henri Frédéric

Sources

Sources

In a conversation with Napoléon Joseph Charles Paul Bonaparte, March 1868, *159*, *180*

In a letter to Karl Wilhelm Ferdinand von Bismarck, September 29, 1838, *105*

Black, Hugo LaFayette
Quoted in Hugo LaFayette Black, *One Man's Stand for Freedom: Mr. Justice Black and the Bill of Rights, A Collection of His Supreme Court Opinions*, 1963, *129*

Blake, William
"Auguries of Innocence," *Poems from the Pickering Manuscript*, c. 1805, Line 53, *174*
"The Marriage of Heaven and Hell," *Proverbs of Hell*, 1790-1793, *94*

Bloch, Arthur McBride
"Matzy's Maxim," *Murphy's Law*, 2003, *170*

Bogue, Haley
In a conversation with Brogan Lee Fullmer, *88*

Boileau-Despreaux, Nicholas
L'art poétique, 1674, *4*

Bonaventure, Saint
Conferences on the Gospel of John, *161*

Bonhoeffer, Dietrich
In a letter to Eberhard Bethge, July 21, 1944, *50*

Boorstin, Daniel Joseph
"A Case of Hypochondria," *Newsweek*, July 6, 1970, *48*

Bose, Partha Sarathi
Alexander the Great's Art of Strategy, 2003, *135*

Boulding, Kenneth Ewart
"The Entropy Trap," *Bulletin of the Atomic Scientists*, September 1970, *32*
Ecodynamics: a new theory of societal evolution, 1979, *57*

Bowen, Elizabeth Dorthea Cole
The House in Paris, 1935, *174*

Bradley, Francis Herbert
Aphorisms, 1930, *23*, *97*

Braude, Jacob Morton
Speaker's desk book of quips, quotes, and anecdotes, number 516, 1955, *21*

Braun, Dr. Wernher Magnus Maximilian von
Quoted in Reader's Digest, *Quotable Quotes*, 1997, *2*

Bright, John
Ascribed comment on Benjamin Disraeli, *147*

Brillat-Savarin, Anthelme
La physiologie du gout, 1825, *82*

Broadhurst, Henry
"To the Celebrated Beauties of the British Court," c. 1700, *136*

Brontë, Charlotte
Villette, chapter 36, 1853, *107*

Brougham, Henry Peter, 1st Baron Brougham and Vaux
Quoted in *The Present State of the Law*, Febrauary 7, 1828, *48*

Broun, Heywood
Quoted in James A. Michener, *Sports in America*, 1976, *158*

Browne, Sir Thomas
Christian Morals, 1716, *177*

Browning, Robert
"Bishop Blougram's Apology", *88*
Apollo and the Fates, prologue, *161*

Henry, Patrick
    In an address to the Virginia Convention, May 23, 1775, *68*
Heraclitus
    Fragments, c. 500 B.C., *92*
    On the Universe, line 21, *24*
Herbert, George
    "The Church Porch," *The Temple*, stanza 5, 1633, *160*
    Jacula Prudentum, 1651, *65*, *114*
        number 141, *70*
        number 153, *125*
        number 390, *41*
        number 524, *176*
        number 652, *106*
        number 723, *159*
Herold, Jean Christopher
    Bonaparte in Egypt, 1962, *115*
Herrick, Robert
    The End, 1648, *3*
Heschel, Abraham Joshua
    The Insecurity of Freedom: Essays on Human Existence, 1967, *28*
Hesiod
    Works and Days, line 1, 698, *172*
Hesse, Herman
    Demian: The Story of Emil Sinclair's Youth, 1919, *84*
    Siddartha, Govinda, 1922, *186*
Hightower, Cullen
    Quoted in Reader's Digest, *Quotable Quotes*, 1997, *136*
Hildegard, Saint
    In a conversation with Frederick Barbarossa, *79*
Hill, Napoleon
    You Can Work Your Own Miracles, 1971, *3*
Hillary, Sir Edmund Percival
    Ascribed to, *3*
Hillman, James
    Ascribed to, *151*
Hitchcock, Jane Stanton
    Ascribed to, *93*
Hitchens, Christopher Eric
    "Terrorism: Notes Toward a Definition," November 18, 2002, *169*
Hobbes, John Oliver
    Wisdom of the Wise, 1900, *52*
Hodgson, Ralph
    The Skylark and Other Poems, page 80, 1958, *66*
Hoffer, Eric
    The Ordeal of Change, 1963, *14*, *135*
    The Passionate State of Mind and other Aphorisms, 1954
        page 110, *57*
        page 130, *39*
        page 21, *95*
        page 217, *52*

Sources

Leverson, Ada
  Love's Shadow, 1908, *5*
  Tenterbooks, chapter 7, 1912, *189*
Lewis, Cecil Day
  The Poet's Task: an Inaugural Lecture Delivered Before the University of Oxford on 1 June 1951, 1951, *192*
Lewis, Clive Staples
  Mere Christianity, book 3, chapter 8, 1952, *140*
  Paraphrasing William Law, "An Appeal to All Who Doubt," "Slip of the Tongue," *The Weight of Glory*, 1965, *76*
Lichfield, Richard
  The Trimming of Thomas Nashe, 1597, *137*
Lichtenberg, Georg Christoph
  "Notebook J," c. 1791, *123*
  "Notebook L," c. 1791, *18*
  Aphorisms, 1799, *95, 111, 186*
  Ascribed to, *86, 133, 179*
  Quoted in Joseph Peter Stern, *Lichtenberg: A Doctrine of Scattered Occasions: Reconstructed from his Aphorisms and Reflections*, *56*
  Quoted in W.H. Auden. *A Certain World: A Common Place Book*, 1970, *18*
Liebling, Abbott Joseph
  "Do You Belong in Journalism?" *New Yorker*, May 4, 1960, *192*
Lincoln, Abraham
  Ascribed to, *135*
  Quoted in Francis Bicknell Carpenter, *Six months at the White House with Abraham Lincoln: the story of a picture*, 1867, *178*
Linkin Park
  "A Place for My Head," *Hybrid Theory*, 2000, *86*
Locke, John
  An Essay Concerning Human Understanding, 1690, *175*
Lodge, David John
  The British Museum is Falling Down, 1965, *111*
Logau, Friedrich von, Freiherr von Logau
  "Retribution," *Poetic Aphorisms*, 1654, *76*
London, Jack
  "Editor's Note" by Douglas Brinkley, in Hunter S. Thompson, *The Proud Highway Saga of a Desperate Southern Gentleman, 1955-1957*, 1997, *98*
Longfellow, Henry Wadsworth
  "Michael Angelo" poetical fragment, *28*
  "The Legend Beautiful," part 2, The Theologian's Tale, *Tales of a Wayside Inn*, 1863, *76*
  Kavanagh, book 1, chapter 1, 1849, *100*
  Morituri Salutamus, stanza 9, 1875, *181*
Los Angeles Times, *112*
Louis XIV
  Quoted in Vincent Cronin, *Louis XIV*, 1965, *74*
Lowell, James Russell
  "Cambridge Thirty Years Ago," *Literary Essays*, volume 1, 1890, *6*
  A Fable for Critics, 1848, *33*
  In an address on democracy, Birmingham, England, October 6, 1884, *95*
  My Study Windows, 1871, *137*

Luce, Clare Booth Luce
  Wit and Wisdom of Famous American Women, 1986, *69*
Lucretius
  De Rerum Natura, c. 30 B.C.
    book 3, line 55, *38*
    book 5, *29*
Lynch, Nicole
  In a conversation with Brogan Lee Fullmer, *176*
Lynes, Jun., Joseph Russell
  Ascribed to, *150*
  In an address to the American Association of Advertising Agencies, April 25, 1963,
    15
MacDiarmid, Hugh
  "Sayings of the Week," *Observer*, March 29, 1953, *192*
MacDonald, George
  Annals of a Quiet Neighborhood, 1872, *71*
Machiavelli, Niccolò
  The Prince, 1517, *41, 61, 67, 81, 92, 95, 101, 135, 181*
Mackenzie, Norman Ian
  The escape from Elba: the fall and flight of Napoleon, 1814-1815, 70
Mackenzie, Sir Compton
  Literature in My Time, chapter 22, 1933, *189*
MacLeod, Fiona
  Quoted in John Boyd-Carpenter, *Way of Life: The Memoirs of John Boyd-Carpenter*,
    1980, *125*
Macnaughton, John
  Ascribed to, 25
MacPhail, Agnes Campbell
  In an address to Ottawa Ladies' College, 1924, *6*
Madison, James
  Federalist Papers, number 51, February 6, 1788, *79*
Mailer, Norman Kingsley
  Writers at Work, 3rd series, *13*
Malcolm X
  Ascribed to, *71*
Mallarmé, Stéphane
  "A Throw of the Dice Will Never Abolish Chance," 1907, *21*
Mallet, Robert
  Apostilles, 1972, *15*
  Ascribed to, *125*
Mandela, Nelson Rolihlahla
  Quoted in Arline B. Tehan, "The Father of a Nation: Going Beyond Myth, Biography
    Captures Mandela in His Humanness, Greatness," *The Hartford Courant*, January
    16, 2000, *150*
Manikan, Ruby
  "Sayings of the Week," *Observer*, March 30, 1947, on a theme by Bishop Fenelon's
    treatise of the education of girls, *49*
Mann, Paul Thomas
  "Tonio Kröger," *Death in Venice*, 1903, *114*
  In a letter to Hans Mayer, 1950, *5*
  The Magic Mountain, 1924, *123*

Pliny the Younger
  Letters, book 2, letter 15, *46*
Plutarch
  Ascribed to, *135*
Pollard, John Garland
  A connotary: Definitions not found in dictionaries, collected from the sayings of the wise and otherwise, 1935, *42*
Pope, Alexander
  Epilogue to the Satires, Dialogue 2, 1738, *61*
  Moral Essays, Epistle II "On the Characters of Women," 1735, *189*
  Quoted in Jonathan Swift, *Miscellanies*, 1727 "Thoughts on Various Subjects, Moral and Diverting," October 1706, *39, 83, 148, 179*
Porter, Michael Eugene
  "What is Strategy," *Harvard Business Review*, page 70, November—December 1996, *42*
Post, Emily
  Ascribed to, *117*
Postman, Neil
  "Introduction," *The Disappearance of Childhood*, 1982, *27*
Pound, Ezra
  "Warning," *ABC of Reading*, 1934, *134*
Prescott, W.B.
  Ascribed to, *128*
Priestley, Joseph
  Ascribed to, *166*
Prior, Matthew
  Upon This Passage in Scaligerana, 1697, *160*
Proust, Valentin Louis Georges Eugène Marcel
  In Search of Lost Time, *91*
    The Fugitive, 1925, *146*
    The Past Recaptured, 1927, *151*
    Time Regained, 1927, *5*
    Within a Budding Grove, 1919, *42, 91, 114*
  Maxims, 1948, *178*
    number 091, *60*
    number 279, *74*
Proverbs, The
  13:11, *184*
  13:12, *44*
  13:20, *187*
  13:3, *167*
  14:20, *184*
  14:7, *103*
  16:18, *140*
  22:24-25, *11*
Radford, Arthur William
  "Admiral," in "Man Behind the Power," *Time*, February 25, 1957, *42*
Rand, Ayn
  The Ayn Rand Letter, 1971, *183*
Ransome, Arthur Mitchell

Quoted in André Gide, *In Memorium, Oscar Wilde,* 1910, *73*
The Critic as Artist, 1891, *13, 101, 144, 168*
The Importance of Being Ernest, 1895, *127*
The Picture of Dorian Gray, 1891, *6, 9, 36, 44, 53, 56, 62, 64, 112, 118, 126, 128*
The Wit and Humor of Oscar Wilde, 1959, *33*
Wilder, Thornton Niven
   The Bridge of San Luis Rey, 1927, *115*
   The Skin of Our Teeth, 1942, *126*
Williams, Charles Walter Stansby
   Symposium on "What the Cross Means to Me," 1943, *19*
Williams, Kenneth
   "Preface" to *Acid Drops,* 1980, *143*
Williams, Tennessee
   "Reflections on a Revival of a Controversial Fantasy," *New York Times,* May 15, 1960, *110*
   In an interview with Studs Terkel, 1961, *51*
Willson, Robert Meredith
   The Music Man, 1957, *146*
Wilmot, John, 2nd Earl of Rochester
   A Satire Against Mankind, line 20, 1675, *112*
Wilson, James Harold, Baron Rievaulx
   Observer, January 11, 1970, *163*
Winner, Robert Michael
   Winner Takes All: A Life of Sorts, 2004, *158*
Winters III, Jonathan Harshman
   Quoted in Reader's Digest, *Quotable Quotes,* 1997, *126, 163*
Wittgenstein, Ludwig Josef Johann
   Ascribed to, *124*
   Tractatus Logico-Philosophicus, page 148, 1922, *193*
Wodehouse, Sir Pelham Grenville
   The Man Upstairs, 1914, *144*
Wolf, David T.
   In a conversation with Robert Byrne, *15*
Wollstonecraft, Mary
   A Vindication of the Rights of Woman: with Strictures on Political and Moral Subjects, chapter 9, 1792, *5*
Woolf, Virginia
   Writer's Diary, entry for August 13, 1921, 1954, *67*
Wotton, Sir Henry
   A Woman's Heart, 1651, *115*
Wright, Gordon
   Ascribed to, *152*
Wright, Steven Alexander
   In a comedy routine, *184*
Wrigley, Jun., William
   Reader's Digest, July 1940, *20*
Wylie, Ida Alexa Ross
   Ascribed to, *131*
Yeats, William Butler
   Ascribed to, *160*

Sources

Yeats-Brown, Francis
  Reader's Digest, February 1940, *112*
Yevtushenko, Yevgeny Alexandrovich
  "People Were Laughing Behind a Wall," translated by George Reavey. 1963, *99*
Young, Edward
  Love of Fame, satire 1, line 89, 1728, *143*
  Night Thoughts, 1745
    Night 1
      line 390, *187*
      line 393, *172*
    Night 4
      line 233, *76*
    Night 5
      line 177, *76*
      line 661, *48*
Yourcenar, Marguerite
  "Saeculum Aureum," *Memoirs of Hadrian,* 1951, *13*
Zinn, Howard
  Terrorism and War, 2002, *170*

"Some for renown, on scraps of learning dote, and think they grow immortal as they quote."

-Edward Young, 1683-1765

61681127R00164

Made in the USA
Lexington, KY
16 March 2017